CW00427861

WHAT WE BELIEVE

GATEWAY CHURCH VISION & VALUES

By Matthew Hosier

Contents

WELCOME TO WHAT WE BELIEVE

What We Believe is an introduction to the things that Gateway Church believes and is passionate about. It is built around our twelve core values and commitments. These are the things that give shape to how we are seeking to live out the Christian story in the power of the Spirit in Poole and Bournemouth in the early 21st century.

What We Believe is an introduction to Gateway and not the whole story. You will only discover the whole story by deciding to fully immerse yourself in the life of the church community. What We Believe will help you decide whether or not you want to do this.

Working through the What We Believe course does not commit you to membership of Gateway Church, but it is a requirement for those wishing to become members.

How to use this book

There are three ways you can use this book:

A good way

If you are not an enthusiastic reader, just stick to reading the twelve 'Snapshot' summaries of our values and commitments on **p.9**, and watch the videos that accompany this book. Then dip into the rest of the book as and when you have questions or want to discover more. At the end of the book is a section titled 'Thinking About It' which contains a number of questions designed to help clarify areas where you need to grow spiritually, and highlight things you might want to talk about with us. Take your time to answer these questions. Be honest and let the Spirit work in your heart as your think things through.

A better way

Do No 1, but also read all the way through this book. Each section of this book is fairly short so you might want to race through it all in one go, but it would probably be better to read one section each day over a couple of weeks. Take it slowly, think about it, and make a list of questions you might have.

The best way

Do No 2, with one or more other people. We usually learn most from discussing things with others, so working through this book and the videos with someone else would be a great way to get into the material. If you then want to do some more study, there is a list of recommended books on **p.109** which represent well the things we believe.

Let's get started!

A Brief History of Gateway Church

In 1925, twenty-one followers of Jesus gathered on the site of what would become our church building at Alder Road to pray Alder Road Baptist Church into existence. Their vision: "To build a chapel, usual or convenient for carrying on the work of a Christian Church." 1925 feels a world away now, but we still carry that original vision to see the church flourish in Poole and beyond. Nearly a century on there have been many changes in our town and in our church (including a change of name) but we are still committed to telling the story of what Jesus has done for us in our local community, across Poole and Bournemouth, and to the ends of the earth.

Some of the key milestones for us in more recent years include:

The Vision

"To build a chapel, usual or convenient for carrying on the work of a Christian Church."
- 1925

Connecting in heart and mission

While Alder Road was founded as a Baptist Church, and we continue to be a member of the Baptist Union, our primary relationship has been with Newfrontiers, becoming part of the Newfrontiers family of churches in the late 1980's.

Newfrontiers was founded and led by Terry Virgo and was born out of the charismatic renewal of the early 1970's. Terry had a powerful personal experience of the Spirit which set off a chain of events in how he understood Christ's purpose for the church – such things as an expectation of the use of spiritual gifts by followers of Jesus; having a team of elders, rather than a solitary pastor, leading local churches; and the role of the 'Ephesians 4' gifts of apostles, prophets, evangelists and pastor-teachers who serve across churches. Over time an increasing number of churches began to look to Terry and the team that grew around him for apostolic leadership, and these churches eventually formed a family known as Newfrontiers.

In 2011 Terry, now in his 70's, stepped back from the leadership of Newfrontiers and a number of other men and their teams were recognised as carrying apostolic authority in the Newfrontiers family. These men were given freedom to grow their own families of churches, and to adopt new names for the groups of churches they work with. At Gateway we are now connected to Commission, which is led by Guy Miller from Citygate Church in Bournemouth, as well as remaining in close connection with other branches of the Newfrontiers family.

Local leadership

In January 2008 I moved to Poole, with Grace and our four daughters. Previously I had been leading New Community Church, Sidcup. Grace and I had moved to Sidcup within a year of getting married, in order to be with David Holden who was leading the church at that time. I spent two years serving the church in a full-time, unpaid position, shadowing David and attending a theology course at Spurgeon's College. I was then employed as the church youth worker, was recognised as an elder, and eventually led the church for seven years. After thirteen years in Sidcup we felt it was time to move on, and – quite unexpectedly! – the Lord led us to Poole.

When I came to Alder Road the church was being led by four elders, all of whom had full time jobs outside the church, but in August 2010 Jon & Vicki Clark and their children moved from Putney, where Jon had been leading the Community Church, for Jon to join the Gateway staff team. Since then we have been seeking to grow and strengthen all our leadership teams. Richard Stamp joined the staff team in August 2011, and we appointed our first deacons in November 2011. A growing elder team now leads Gateway, with an excellent deacon team serving pastorally across the church, and others leading in various areas.

A change of name

When I moved to Poole I felt that it would be helpful for us to have change of name. I came with a strong sense of being called to reach the 400,000 people in the 'South East Dorset Conurbation' rather than just a small parish around our church building, so the name 'Alder Road Baptist' felt a little restricting. However, making a change happened rather quicker than I had anticipated when in July 2008 a prophet from Canada was at a meeting in Bournemouth and prophesied over some members of Alder Road who were there: "I believe God recommissions you tonight to be a mighty army in the community, God wants you to touch Poole by the power of the Holy Spirit and be a gateway into the Kingdom of God."

While I was not at the meeting myself, as soon as I heard this prophecy the name 'Gateway' leapt out at me and in September 2008 we changed our name to that.

More meetings

With limited space and a growing congregation, in January 2009 we began running two services at Alder Road on a Sunday morning. This served us very well, but we were also discussing, and becoming increasingly committed to, having meetings in more than one location. In seeking God's direction for us, and in thinking about the town in which we live, we came to the conclusion that multiple meetings/locations was a better fit for us at this time than seeking to buy a big warehouse-type building to meet in.

In response to this, in April 2013 we launched a second meeting at Poole Quay. Our hope and expectation is that in the coming years we will add more meetings and more locations. This creates some complexity in leadership and oversight, but is also a wonderful way of multiplying leaders, creating space for more people to serve, and helping us to connect with our local communities.

Forward, together

We are very optimistic about the future of the church! We believe Jesus is building his church. There are times when the church suffers apparent setbacks, but because God's plan is to display his multi-coloured wisdom and glory through the church (Eph 3:10,21) we are confident that the church has a brilliant future. This means we are full of faith about what Jesus is doing at Gateway, and together we want to step into all that he has planned for us. Why not come with us?!

> "I believe God recommissions you tonight to be a mighty army in the community, God wants you to touch Poole by the power of the Holy Spirit and be a gateway into the Kingdom of God."
>
> - Keith Hazel, July 2008

Snapshots:
Summing up our vision and values

Snapshot 1: We are a people called into an adventure of faith

We believe that the instruction Jesus gave to his first followers to, go to all nations to make disciples, applies to us still. Our mission is to communicate the message of Jesus as effectively as we can to as many people as we can. Practically, this means that we encourage all church members to see themselves as missionaries, who are called to make Jesus known wherever they are. In turn, this means we don't run a separate 'evangelism program' – the church is the missionary agency, and her members are the missionaries. The role of the elders is to equip and encourage the whole church to be together on mission. We also have a passion for mission beyond our local communities in the UK, and overseas. Church planting through the Newfrontiers family of churches is our primary focus for this.

To read more, turn to p. 12

Snapshot 2: We are a people called to live in purity

'Purity' and 'holiness' are Bible words, but they are words we often have a problem with. To our ears 'purity' can sound conservative and stodgy – something rather boring and dull. By contrast, when we hear 'sin' we tend to think that something fun and relatively harmless is implied – something like an extra helping of chocolate cake. As followers of Jesus we need to rewire our hearing and understand what these words really represent, because in reality sin is more like eating sewage than chocolate cake and purity is about life and health and happiness rather than something constraining.

To read more, turn to p. 20

Snapshot 3: We are a people called to live compassionately

The church should not shut itself away from the troubles of the world. The sound of war, famine, sickness and death should rattle in our ears. But rather than provoking us to despair, this sound encourages us into action. This means we offer support and care to those who are suffering because of their faithfulness to the name of Jesus. It also means we are not blind to the social needs in the communities around us. We want to make the love and grace of God known to those who are sick, oppressed, poor and unjustly treated, and this has very practical implications for how we use our time and resources. Living compassionately does not simply mean that we are big on charity, but that we are committed to living in a way that demonstrates the reality of Christ's mercy towards us.

To read more, turn to p. 30

Snapshot 4: We are a people transformed by the grace of God

Our relationship with Jesus is entirely dependent on his grace to us. We cannot earn God's love or favour, but are freely given it. This amazing grace liberates us, and makes us confident and secure. This grace is the defining experience in all our actions and relationships. Grace declares that God's love for you is complete, unchanging and unconditional. You are accepted just as you are! Once you have been justified by faith you are completely accepted because of the righteousness of Jesus that has been given to you. You can't improve God's love for you. You can't reduce God's love for you. Grace makes for motivated, inspired Christians serving God and each other out of delight and joy, and not out of fear or bondage!

To read more, turn to p. 38

Snapshot 5: We are a people who joyfully recognize the sovereignty of God

We are confident that God is working out his purpose in the world, the church and our individual lives. This confidence brings us into joy as we see how we are part of something of universal and eternal scope. It also brings us into peace as we can trust Jesus to do what is right.

To read more, turn to p. 44

Snapshot 6: We are a people committed to generosity

Jesus has been very good to us! In response we want to live as generous people, giving of our time, energy and resources to bring blessing to other people. Practically, this means we teach tithing (giving away ten per cent of our income) as the starting point for financial giving by church members and we constantly push back against both materialism and financial meanness masquerading as good stewardship.

To read more, turn to p. 52

Snapshot 7: We are committed to growing

We have a theological and philosophical commitment to growth. We understand the kingdom of God to be advancing, and the gospel to be fruitful. This means we expect the local church to experience growth as part of its normal life – both in terms of growth in knowledge and love for Jesus, and numerical growth.

To read more, turn to p. 60

Snapshot 8: We are committed to pastoring

We are committed to a model of church leadership that sees elders remaining in close contact with the flock they have been given responsibility to shepherd, with a deacon team assisting in this. While it is not possible for any one elder to have genuine connection with everyone who is a part of Gateway, an elder and deacon team and multisite structure help ensure no-one slips through the net. At the same time, growth is not corked, because rather than seeing growth as a negative that will result in the elders being out of touch with the people, growth is seen as an opportunity to start a new meeting or location and to appoint more elders and deacons.

To read more, turn to p. 68

Snapshot No.9: We are committed to team

We are called to be together on a mission and want all that we do as a church to reflect God's priority for team. This affects the way we understand leadership in the church, and the role that every church member has as a member of the team.

To read more, turn to p. 76

Snapshot 10: We are committed to community

A commitment to community means being genuinely immersed in the neighbourhoods we serve and concerned for their wellbeing. This love for our wider communities flows out of the community of the church, which begins with our communion with God. We want to do whatever we can to guard and build community. This means learning to be faithful to one another in all our relationships.

To read more, turn to p. 82

Snapshot 11: We are committed to the city

While committed to our local communities we do not want to become parochial, but to have a sense of responsibility for the whole 'city' we live in. Being a multisite church with each congregation being organically connected to the other congregations the whole church is kept focussed on the task of reaching the whole city. In the end, our aim is to build a large church, not just small ones!

To read more, turn to p. 90

Snapshot 12: We are committed to preaching

We are committed to preaching because we believe it to be God's method for the proclamation of the word. Because we are committed to growth and to team we want to develop elders who are able to preach in their own right to their own congregations. Because we are committed to pastoral care and community we want preaching to be by elders who are part of that community and understand it. We believe preaching is powerful and is an act of spiritual warfare. Submitting ourselves to listen to preaching week by week not only informs us, but is a means of submitting to Jesus and rejecting the devil!

To read more, turn to p. 96

a people called into an

Commitment #1:
We are a people called into an adventure of faith

Adventurous faith means understanding the character of God[1]

We want the values that we hold as a church to reflect the nature and character of God. Fundamental to our Christian faith is the understanding that there is only one God, but that God is Trinity: Father, Son and Holy Spirit. There is no division within God, and he is never confused about his plans and purpose – his mission is clear! At the same time, God is working out his plan and purpose in the context of community, as Father, Son and Spirit dwell and delight in one another eternally.

God's plan is to gather all his people to himself and in order to accomplish this the Trinity had to get missional! Jesus was sent by the Father and empowered by the Spirit in order that all God's people might be brought into relationship with him. This is a relationship of love, in which we are drawn into community with God. Just before he went to the cross, Jesus prayed like this:

> O righteous Father, even though the world does not know you, I know you, and these know that you have sent me. I made known to them your name, and I will continue to make it known, that the love with which you have loved me may be in them, and I in them.
>
> (John 17:25-26)

The prayer of Jesus was that his followers might be drawn into community with his Father and himself! This relationship that God calls us to defines what the church is to be: Community on Mission! In this community the love we feel for the lost, and for each other, flows out of the love the Father has for us, in Jesus Christ. The Holy Spirit unifies the community in this love, and empowers us for mission!

This is all amazing. However, at times, rather than being community on mission, it can feel as though mission and community are pulling in opposite directions because 'Community' tends to resist change, while 'Mission' always creates it! Sometimes, those who have been part of a church a long time can feel disgruntled when new people come in. It can be challenging if the worship style changes. It can be unsettling if someone new is sitting in 'my' seat! It can be difficult if friends you once had leave to go on mission elsewhere, and new people come in who you do not know.

The apparent tension between community and mission is not new! In Acts 6:1-7 we read about these kind of tensions in the first church, in Jerusalem, and how it was resolved. This was a church that did community, caring for those who were in need. It was also a church that did mission, which meant it was growing rapidly, and there came a point where one part of the church thought they were being excluded from community by another. By the grace of God, the apostles fixed this problem, and keep the church moving forward in both community and mission. Here is how they did it:

---

1   Thanks to PJ Smyth, from Godfirst Church, Johannesburg, for help with this section.

Acts 6:1-7

Now in these days when the disciples were increasing in number, a complaint by the Hellenists arose against the Hebrews because their widows were being neglected in the daily distribution. ² And the twelve summoned the full number of the disciples and said, "It is not right that we should give up preaching the word of God to serve tables. ³ Therefore, brothers, pick out from among you seven men of good repute, full of the Spirit and of wisdom, whom we will appoint to this duty. ⁴ But we will devote ourselves to prayer and to the ministry of the word." ⁵ And what they said pleased the whole gathering, and they chose Stephen, a man full of faith and of the Holy Spirit, and Philip, and Prochorus, and Nicanor, and Timon, and Parmenas, and Nicolaus, a proselyte of Antioch. ⁶ These they set before the apostles, and they prayed and laid their hands on them.

⁷ And the word of God continued to increase, and the number of the disciples multiplied greatly in Jerusalem, and a great many of the priests became obedient to the faith.

They didn't abandon mission

The apostles were committed to preaching the word (Acts 6:2) and this was meant to result in the increase of the word (v7). The tensions within the community were not going to be solved by limiting the size of the community, and the apostles didn't lose sight of the ball on this one.

They were honest

In this situation the apostles didn't try to pretend that there wasn't a problem – they kept their ears open, heard what people had to say, and initiated a solution. This provides us with a good model for reporting and fixing problems: the church didn't go on the attack against their leaders – after all, the leaders were not in sin – it was a problem caused by mission. Also, the apostles did not feel compelled to fix the problem themselves, but delegated authority to others to do so. Together, the church and its leaders worked the problem through.

They increased organisation

Sometimes there can be a perception that being organised and having systems is somehow unspiritual. From this account in Acts 6 we can see that this is not the case. There was a practical problem, that needed practical solutions, by spiritual men! As we grow in mission we also need to grow in organisation.

They increased the number of leaders

The solution to the problem was found in more leaders – whatever we do in church life requires leaders! Mission needs leaders, because the problem isn't the harvest but lack of labourers. And community needs leaders, who can help build community like good parents build a family.

They shared responsibility

In order to solve the problem at hand, more people took more responsibility. As the old joke goes: in a bacon-and-egg breakfast, what's the difference between the Chicken and the Pig? *The Chicken is involved, but the Pig is committed!* In order to resolve the tension between mission and community we need people who are committed, not just involved.

They acted in faith

One of the men chosen to help fix the problem was Stephen, who was noted for being full of faith (v5). Our church needs people with faith, who help the whole church feel faith. Faith is infectious!

They were led by the Spirit

Stephen and the others were full of the Spirit (v3). Gateway needs spiritual people! In order to be effective in mission and community we need to keep experiencing the power of the Spirit.

They grew in hospitality

The Jerusalem church demonstrated hospitality both by caring for those who were part of the church and by reaching out to those outside the church. We want to be a hospitable people!

The result

At Jerusalem a commitment to quality (growing in community) was married to a commitment to quantity (growing in mission). They were a missional community, where mission and community were friends, in a symbiotic relationship, not rivals, pulling the church apart.

Adventurous faith means understanding our culture

If I relocated to another country, I would want to do all I could to understand the culture of the place I was moving to in order to be able to connect with the people who live there. Different cultures look at life from a different angle. For example, if I were in Japan and wanted to be really offensive to someone I might say, *misokkasu*, which means scum of soya paste. This is how missionaries need to think – not how to insult people (!) but how being an effective missionary often means doing things differently from how you do them at home. For example, if I were going to a muslim country I would not put my Bible on the floor, as in Islamic culture this is a sign of disrespect.

This is what we call contextualization, and to be effective in mission we need to contextualize. Ultimately, the question we need to keep asking ourselves is, "How can I most effectively help people see the truth of God in Christ?" Of course, Jesus himself is the master and model of contextualization: In the Incarnation God took on human flesh, and lived as a Jew in occupied first century Judea, just like any other first century Jew.
The apostle Paul was also a master of contextualization, and the account of his time in Athens (Acts 17:16-34) gives us a model of how to contextualize without compromise:

Paul demonstrated love and distress
Paul loved the Athenians enough to go to them, understand them, and seek to win them, but he was distressed at the sin of the city (v16). This is the missionary tension – a tension we should feel. We should not be so 'loving' that we are subsumed within the culture, nor so hostile we withdraw from the culture. Put another way…

Paul was 'in' but not 'of'
Paul had his head in the culture, but kept his heart pure from the sins of the culture. It is essential that we learn how to keep our hearts *disengaged* from worldly things while being fully *engaged* with worldly people!

Paul knew how to connect and challenge
Being all connection and no challenge is as fruitless as being all challenge and no connection! We all know what it is like to pass a street preacher or have a salesman cold call us and feel no response to their challenge because we have no connection with them. Paul wasn't like this. In the Areopagus he behaved appropriately, observing the conventions of Athenian culture and forming a connection with his listenerer, but he was also uncompromisingly clear in his message.

Paul *connected* with the Athenians by acknowledging their spirituality, philosophy and poetry – he commended what could be commended about their culture. He also *challenged* them by saying idols that their worship of idols demonstrated ignorance (v30).

Paul knew how to contend and contextualize
Jude 3 says that we are to, *Contend for the faith that was once for all delivered to the saints;* while in 1 Corinthians 9:22 Paul writes, *I have become all things to all people, that by all means I might save some.* The gospel is not up for grabs – we must contend for the faith that has been given to us, but at the same time we should contextualise. Very often what this means is that we need to be willing to submit our preferences in order to fit in with others.

This might mean eating food we wouldn't normally choose, or adjusting the way we organise our Sunday meetings, or decorate our building. We should do whatever we can do to in order to contextualize the gospel, but without compromising the gospel!

Paul did this by finding points of connection between himself and the Athenians. For example, he drew attention to the seriousness with which they approached religion (v22) – just as he was serious about his faith. And he deliberately quoted from poetry and philosophy that was culturally important to them. The context in which we are likely to be most fruitful in doing this is with people we can connect with easily because we share their culture. Whatever your social background and interests, God can use you to connect with people who share a similar culture.

Paul studied both the Bible and the culture

Paul *observed* what was happening in Athens (v23), and *reasoned* with them on the basis of scripture (v17). We should think about the messages being communicated in our culture, through the media and entertainment, shops, sport and politics, and then seek to connect the story told us in the Bible to these things.

In order to be able to do this we need to be alert to the pre-suppositions of our culture. There are the underlying beliefs people hold, and the issues they will have with Christianity. In contemporary British culture often the big issues people have can be summarised under three 'S's': Suffering, Science and Sex. We need to be ready to give answers to the questions our culture raises on these issues. (If you need help, two fantastic books are *If God Then What?* by Andrew Wilson, and *The Reason for God* by Tim Keller.)

Paul was ready for a range of responses

Paul was a brilliant missionary, but this by no means meant he got a consistent response! In Athens some mocked, some wanted to hear more, and some believed (vv32-34). In the end however effective we are in communicating our faith we need to be ready for a range of responses, and to trust that in it all God is Sovereign!

a people called to live in

PUR

Commitment #2:
We are a people called to live in purity

How we live matters to Jesus so we want to be a church where people are helped to live life right. Purity is not about legalism, so we don't try to control one another through rules and regulations. Rather, living in a way which is pleasing to our God and Saviour can only happen by His grace, so our desire is to be a grace-filled community. Living a pure life is not easy, so we work hard at being disciples of Jesus at Gateway. We want to have relationships with one another that are strong and which help us become increasingly like Jesus. And we believe in the power of God's Spirit to enable us to live in purity.

Sanctification: Living a pure life

When we become Christians God puts the power within us to overcome sin. We do not simply adjust our lifestyle choices, but die to what we previously were. This is why the apostle Paul writes, *Count yourselves dead to sin but alive to God in Christ Jesus... For sin shall not be your master* (Romans 6:11-14). As those made alive in this way we can never say, "I am completely free from sin", because all of us still do sin, and will do so until we die or Jesus comes again. But (and this is a big but!), neither can we say, "This sin has defeated me. I give up. I will never be able to overcome it." Sometimes when we are struggling with an especially hard temptation it can feel as though we will never overcome it, but by God's grace there is always a way through.

The more Christ-like we become, the more sensitive we will be to the ugliness of sin in our lives and the more we will want to be radical in dealing with it. Jesus earned our sanctification by his death on the cross and it is Jesus who is our example of sanctification as the only man who has lived an entirely sin-free and blameless life. Now God puts his *Holy* Spirit in us to work sanctification in us.

Sanctification does not equal, "let go and let God". Rather, we lay hold of God and allow him to do his work in us. *For if you live according to the sinful nature, you will die; but if by the Spirit you put to death the misdeeds of the body, you will live* (Romans 8:13). Sanctification is something we work at – we cannot be lazy!

While sanctification is clearly something that affects us individually, the New Testament normally sees growth in holiness as being something we do together with our brothers and sisters in Christ. It is holiness that ensures we will act in an appropriate way together and show love and acceptance towards one another. It is growing in sanctification together that enables us to trust other members of the family.

As we grow in sanctification we will find that every part of our being is affected. The attitude of our hearts and the actions of our bodies will be changed and this process of purification will get to work on every aspect of our character. The way we think about things will begin to change. Being sanctified will change the way in which we respond emotionally to other people. It will make us nicer people to be with!

Baptism in water: The sign of our purity

We believe that the biblical basis for baptism is that it is only for those who have already responded in faith to Jesus. Baptism does not save us, but it is a powerful sign and declaration of saving faith, without which we are missing a crucial step in the process of our salvation. Baptism is the mark and evidence of our entrance into the church of Jesus Christ.

bap-tizo

Greek word meaning 'to plunge, dip or immerse'

How should baptism happen? With lots of water! The Greek word *baptizo* means, "to plunge, dip, immerse." There is an expectation in the word itself that the person being baptised is completely immersed in water. In the New Testament accounts of baptism we can see that it always happened where there was lots of water, normally *in* a river. The person getting baptised was not sprinkled but was baptised: plunged, dipped, immersed. This was not because there is some magic about the amount of water used, but because of what the water symbolises.

When we go under the water of baptism it is as if we are dying with Christ, burying our sin with him. When we come out of the water we share in the resurrection of Jesus. Our sin stays buried, but we are made alive. Baptism is a sign of God's judgement upon sin but coming out of the water is a sign that, united with Christ, we pass safely through God's judgement into life. Baptism is an appeal to God; a cry of faith. Non-believers cannot make this appeal! Baptism is for those who make a genuine profession of faith.

Baptism is not *necessary* for salvation but it is part of the normal order of salvation and without baptism we are seriously missing out on God's grace to us. And as baptism is a command of Jesus, it *is* necessary if we are to be obedient to him. Jesus instructed his disciples, *Go and make disciples of all nations, baptising them in the name of the Father and of the Son and of the Holy Spirit* (Matthew 28:19). If we obey Jesus in this command we can expect to receive the blessing that comes with obedience.

Baptism strengthens and encourages our faith. It does this for the one being baptised and also for those who are watching. It is a tangible, physical representation of a spiritual reality. It is far more than merely a symbol. Baptism is a once and for all declaration: "I was a sinner, destined for hell, but now I am declared righteous. I belong to Jesus and will be with him forever!"

Because believers baptism is so crucial it is something we expect of all church members. Sometimes this can be something of a stumbling block for those who have been baptised as infants and want to become members of Gateway. If you are in this category we would love to chat with you about it!

Baptism in the Holy Spirit: Being empowered and equipped to live in purity

In order to live in purity we need to be empowered by the Holy Spirit. Spirit baptism involves empowering and equipping; it is not just a warm feeling. There is a promise of power, because the Spirit is God and God is powerful! When we are baptised in the Spirit we know something has happened to us and we are changed. One of the things we experience is a great assurance that God is our Father. Spirit baptism is also accompanied by an outward expression. It might be that we address God as "*Abba*! Father!" in a way we have never been able to before, and normally there will be a new boldness to witness for Jesus as well as spiritual gifts such as tongues and prophecy.

Baptism in the Spirit should be part of the normal order of salvation. In the book of Acts we see that new believers were always filled with the Spirit, but there was great variety in when this happened. There is no strict pattern that must always be followed as to how and when people receive the Spirit. However, there is an expectation that all believers will be baptised in the Spirit, and ideally conversion, baptism in water and baptism in the Spirit should all happen close together. The exact process by which this happens has often been a point of debate, but we would want all members of Gateway to be able to agree the following five points.[2]

---

2   Thanks to Andrew Wilson, from King's Church Eastbourne, for this summary

1 Baptism in the Spirit in the New Testament is an experienced reality, and results in a visible change in people's lives.

Biblically, it is pretty difficult to argue with this. The very word "baptised", or "drenched", assumes that the subject is aware of the experience, since one cannot reasonably be drenched without knowing it. Jesus clearly promised that the disciples would receive power when the Holy Spirit came upon them and that they would go all over the world as a result (Acts 1:4-8), and compared the experience of receiving the Spirit to someone having rivers of living water flowing from within them (John 7:37-39).

The book of Acts contains multiple accounts of people being baptised in the Spirit (even where the word is not used, it seems clear from texts like Acts 11:15-17 that baptism in the Spirit is what is happening), and in each case there is a clear, visible sign: a rushing wind (2:2), tongues of fire (2:3), speaking in new languages (2:4-11; 10:46; 19:6), declaring the praises of God (2:4-11; 10:46), recovering sight (9:17-18), bold public preaching of the gospel (9:20; cf. 4:8), prophesying (19:6; cf. 13:9-11), and something of such significance that Simon Magus wanted to buy it (8:17-19).

Paul only uses the language of being baptised in the Spirit once (1 Cor 12:13), but it comes in the middle of a chapter all about the use of spiritual gifts in the church, all of which are used publicly and corporately, rather than being things which have no visible demonstration (12:7-11, 28-31). His exhortation to be filled with the Spirit, likewise, anticipates visible results (Eph 5:18-21), and his references to receiving the Spirit associate the experience with a deep, heartfelt assurance of the love and preservation of God (Rom 8:14-17; 2 Cor 1:21-22; Eph 1:13-14) and with the working of miracles (Gal 3:2-5).

Frankly, there is no biblical evidence whatsoever for a baptism in (or receiving of) the Spirit that does not produce significant, demonstrable, powerful results in the lives of individuals and churches.

2 The laying on of hands to receive the Spirit was an important part of Christian initiation and discipleship in the New Testament, although it has often been neglected, misrepresented or even ignored in contemporary churches.

When the Spirit first fell on the Jews (Acts 2:1-4) and on the Gentiles (10:44-47), he fell on them without anyone laying hands on anyone, but in all the other stories in Acts, the laying on of hands was involved in the receiving of the Spirit (8:14-17; 9:10-20; 19:1-7). In two of these cases it was apostles who laid hands on people, but in Saul's case it was Ananias, the nobody *par excellence*, which (among other things) shows that official or institutional authority was not needed to lay hands on people – Ananias is not mentioned anywhere else in scripture, but is an incredibly important figure because of his role in Paul's conversion.

Although the practice was clearly used to set apart apostles (Acts 13:3) and elders (1 Tim 5:22), it was used elsewhere to confer the "gift of God" (2 Tim 1:6), and the writer to the Hebrews includes it as one of the basic Christian teachings everybody knows about, along with repentance, faith, baptism and future resurrection (Heb 6:1-3).

Apparently, in the New Testament period, laying hands on people was something you were meant to do when somebody professed faith in Christ, whether before or after their baptism in water. So the fact that so many churches either do not lay on hands at all, or only do so in the context of "confirmation" (which is something quite different from what we see in Acts), is problematic. The early church laid hands on people as part of Christian initiation – and they expected something significant to happen when they did.

New Testament believers, on receiving the Spirit, were characterised by a combination of assurance, joy, power, spiritual giftedness, evangelistic zeal, perseverance through suffering and fruitfulness.

Again, this one is not especially controversial biblically, although some have put such a wedge between the New Testament period and ours that the expectation for all of these things has diminished somewhat. The important point is that the Spirit-drenched Christian life, in New Testament terms, involves all of these things and not just some of them.

Much modern evangelicalism has, at times, emphasised evangelistic zeal, perseverance and fruitfulness at the expense of spiritual giftedness, joy and power; in charismatic circles, at times, the reverse has happened. But biblically, as far as we can tell, the baptism in (or receiving of) the Spirit produces all of these things. A life without assurance, joy unspeakable, power, spiritual giftedness, evangelistic zeal, perseverance through suffering and fruitfulness was not a Spirit-baptised life at all.

 If such tangible demonstrations of the Spirit's power and presence are not evident in a person's life, something is missing, and needs to be pursued with urgency.

Pastorally, this is where the rubber hits the road. In some traditions, the absence of one or more of the above evidences of the Spirit's work could be seen as normal, since the apostolic age was unusual in the levels of power and spiritual giftedness experienced by believers. In some other traditions, it might be seen as not quite ideal, but something that should be accepted and handed over to the sovereignty of God, on the basis that he decides whether we are given those things or not. For Charismatics, however, there is no hermeneutical, dispensational or covenantal break between the age of the apostles and the twenty-first century, and we should therefore both expect the same results of the Spirit's work that the early church did, and pursue him urgently if they are missing.

The expectation is fundamentally different, for the charismatic; "normal" Christianity is apostolic Christianity, and it is the contemporary church, rather than the first century church, which is the aberration. This does not mean that all Spirit-baptised Christians will speak in languages, prophesy or have healing gifts, but it does mean that such gifts are to be not just accepted, but eagerly desired, by all believers (1 Cor 14:1).

 A one-off experience is not the end of the story, however; believers need to go on being filled with the Holy Spirit, and continue having fresh experiences of his power and transforming work in their lives.

Peter was filled with the Spirit on the day of Pentecost (Acts 2:1-4), but was filled again a while later for boldness (4:8), and then again during their prayer meeting when the building shook (4:31). Saul/Paul was filled with the Spirit when Ananias laid hands on him (9:17), but was filled again when speaking to Elymas (13:9). Nor are these unusual examples: Paul later exhorts the entire Ephesian church to be filled with the Spirit, which means "go on being filled with the Spirit." The imperative is to continue having fresh experiences of the Holy Spirit, and not to see the experience as a past event that cannot be repeated; in that sense it is much more like a sail continually being filled with wind, or a pair of lungs with breath (*pneuma* = Spirit/breath/wind), than a glass being filled with water. The metaphor of drinking (1 Cor 12:13) makes the same point.

How can you be baptised in the Spirit?

Hopefully you will agree with the theology of the Spirit set out above. (If you don't, let's talk!) Practically, then, how can you have this experience? I have found the following process helpful:

Believe that *this is the promise of the Father* to all who believe. The names given to Jesus of "Christ" and "Messiah" both mean "the anointed one." He came to release the anointing of the Spirit upon all the Father's children.

Believe that *this experience is for you personally* – God has not excluded you from his promise.

Have *an expectation of experience*. God loves to move in response to faith. If you have no expectation, you are unlikely to have an experience.

The Spirit is normally given by *the laying on of hands* by another Spirit filled believer. God loves to work through the members of his body and having someone lay hands on us is a clear demonstration that we are open to receive the gift of God.

Finally, *ask*! Jesus said, *If anyone is thirsty, let him come to me and drink* (John 7:37). If you are thirsty for the Spirit ask for this drink, and you will be satisfied.

The reality of eternity: Fuel for purity here and now

Jesus is King! Our hope is that just as Jesus ascended to heaven following his resurrection he will one day return to claim his people and make all things new. We do not know when this will happen, and how it will happen is a matter of great debate amongst Christians. At Gateway we do not take a strong position on the "how" of these events, but we do believe strongly in what their outcome will be: eternal life with Jesus in a new heavens and earth for those who have responded in faith to him in this life; and eternal punishment in hell for those who have rejected him.

In the sixteenth century two young pastors were commissioned to write a series of questions and answers which summarised the Christian faith. What they came up with is known as the Heidelberg catechism. Question 52 asks: *How does Christ's return "to judge the living and the dead" comfort you?*

The answer given is this: *In all my affliction and persecution I may await with head held high the very Judge from heaven who has already submitted himself to the judgement of God for me and has removed all the curse from me. He will cast all his enemies and mine into everlasting condemnation, but he will take me and all his chosen ones to himself into the joy and glory of heaven.*

This is a wonderful statement of what we believe! Jesus has already borne the punishment of God in our place, so no-one need be condemned. But those who remain as enemies of God will be judged and this justice will be right and it will be God glorifying.

The world is in a mess because of the sin of men. The coming judge is the one who will create order and restore what has been destroyed. Those who have put their faith in him can look forward to this day "with head held high." His second coming will bring greater joy than his first. But for those who reject Jesus his second coming will not be good news. Rather than celebrating, for them there will be weeping.

Talking about the reality of hell is not very popular in our culture. But hell is real, and so is the offer of eternal life with Christ in a perfected universe. This should strongly motivate us to share the grace of God with all those we meet. It also fuels the fires of pure living, as we seek to act in a manner now which reflects how we will live eternally.

a people **called** to live

COMPASS

Commitment #3:
We are a people called to live compassionately

The Compassionate Gospel

What was the last thing that stirred you to compassion? Perhaps there has been something on the news that has affected you – a natural disaster or tragedy of war that has moved you. Perhaps there has been something closer to home – a friend or loved one who is in need. Or, perhaps it is a while since anything touched your heart with compassion – in which case you probably need to have some heart surgery, because the gospel has a lot to say about compassion!

We see God's heart of compassion throughout the Old Testament where the people of Israel are given explicit instructions about generosity towards the poor and an attitude of compassion is encouraged. Widows, orphans and foreigners were to be well cared for; when crops were harvested some was to be left behind for the poor to glean; and all debts were to be cancelled regularly.

When Jesus began his ministry he read from the prophet Isaiah to announce what he had come to do:

> *"The Spirit of the Lord is upon me, because he has anointed me to proclaim good news to the poor. He has sent me to proclaim liberty to the captives and recovering of sight to the blind, to set at liberty those who are oppressed, to proclaim the year of the Lord's favour."*
>
> (Luke 4:18-19)

Jesus was the King who was coming to bring *shalom* (God's perfect peace) to the world. Jesus' kingdom would end poverty in all its forms: spiritual, emotional, physical and material.

A compassionate king and his compassionate people

If the kingdom Jesus is ushering in will be a compassionate place, it must also be the work of his servants to act compassionately. Jesus himself made this plain in the famous parable of the sheep and the goats, found in Matthew 25:31-46. In this parable we see how compassion works.

The Father's compassion for us

God's compassion is wonderfully seen in that he brings into his family people like us! This is not a casual thing, but God's planned inheritance, for the Father's blessed people. Those who are *blessed by my Father* (v34) receive a great inheritance: the kingdom of God and all that he has! All of us could have been cast aside, like a cloud of flies to be swatted away, but God brings humans into a place of honour.

Remarkably, God's children are regarded with the same honour as the Son. We have been brought out of poverty into riches, so the primary Christian response to God is gratitude: He has been compassionate to us and we worship him! Our attitude to others must also be shaped by the mercy we have received.

Compassion for the family

There can be no real relationship with the king without relationship with his family. The evidence of our membership of the family is the extent to which we honour the family, because this is they way in which we honour God. As members of God's family we are to live in a way now that demonstrates the kingdom to come. In fact, the evidence of the kingdom among us should provoke the world to envy so they say, "We want this too." This means we should never be embarrassed about doing good to the family.

In Galatians 6:10 Paul writes, *as we have opportunity, let us do good to everyone, and especially to those who are of the household of faith.* We are meant to care for others in the church, and we are meant to care for Christians who are suffering, even when we do not know them personally, because we are part of the same family.

Compassion for the world

The poet Shelley said, "I could believe in Jesus, if only he did not drag behind him his leprous bride, the church." Sadly, many people feel this way, even if they do not express the sentiment quite so eloquently. Many shameful things have been done in the name of the church over the centuries because when the church forgets who she is and mirrors the world she becomes leprous. However, the true church is founded by the compassion of the Father and compassion flows out of her. Rather than being leprous this church is being *made holy and without blemish* (Eph 5:27). In fact, far from being leprous, the true church cares for the leper! This is because the kingdom compassion of the church spills out beyond the family into the wider community. When we pray "Your kingdom come" we are really looking for the kingdom to be demonstrated through us!

Compassion for the poor

After Hurricane Katrina, which caused devastation to New Orleans in 2005, former deputy leader of the Labour Party Roy Hattersley wrote,

> *The Salvation Army has been given a special status as provider-in-chief of American disaster relief. But its work is being augmented by all sorts of other groups. Almost all of them have a religious origin and character. Notable by their absence are teams from rationalist societies, free thinkers' clubs and atheists' associations - the sort of people who…regard [religion] as a positive force for evil.*

What Hattersley was observing was the fact that Christian faith always has a compassionate edge. There is no question that Christians should be concerned for the poor, but the obvious next question is, Who *are* the poor? And how can we *help* the poor? This is an immensely complicated subject, but at Gateway we have tried to develop a grid through which we can answer these kinds of questions, and most effectively focus our desire to help those who are poor.

We understand that poverty is a wider problem than just material poverty. Poverty affects every aspect of being human, because human rebellion against God has caused poverty to enter all our relationships. We were made for relationship and wherever relationship is broken we see a form of poverty:[3]

---

3   The books *When Helping Hurts* by Steve Corbett & Brian Fikkert and *Toxic Charity* by Robert Lupton have helped us develop the following framework and supply some of the illustrations

- *Relationship with God:* This is the primary relationship we were made for as we were created to glorify God and enjoy him forever. If our relationship with God is not restored we are in fundamental poverty, slaves to sin and death.
- *Relationship with self:* This is different from the contemporary concept of self-esteem – rather than looking within ourselves and seeking something to esteem, real 'self-health' happens when we look outside ourselves and see the dignity and worth we have as those who have been made in the image of God. A failure to see ourselves in this way leads us into poverty of emotion.
- *Relationship with others:* No man is an island and if we are not in good relationship with others we are poor.
- *Relationship with the rest of creation:* God gave human beings a mandate to rule creation and to be fruitful. When we do not enjoy this rule and fruitfulness we are poor.

This wider definition of poverty recognises that all human beings need to be delivered from poverty and only God can do this. Much poverty relief fails because it does not recognise poverty in its full breadth. Those who are non-poor materially can easily develop a God-complex when they assist the materially poor, but this simply brings the materially rich into greater poverty of relationships with others.

Conversely, the feelings of inferiority experienced by the materially poor can keep them in poverty even as they are being practically helped. We do not want to be part of poverty relief that harms both the materially poor and non-poor!

Effective poverty alleviation

To truly relieve poverty we must begin by restoring relationships – with God, with self, with others, and with the rest of creation. This means we seek to work with the poor, utilising the assets they already possess and help them find reconciliation with God, others, creation and themselves.

One way we have found helpful in assessing the level of need, the response required, and the framework within which to operate in serving the poor is to think in three distinct, yet overlapping phases:

Phase I: RELIEF

In the relief phase, there is an immediate need, which needs to be met. For example, in the story of the Good Samaritan, Jesus highlights a relief phase response to poverty. A man lies beaten in the street, and the Samaritan stops to offer immediate assistance without question. In this scenario it would be a missiological absurdity for the Samaritan to consider ways to change the system that created the beaten man. The man is lying in a ditch covered in blood and needs immediate help! The Samaritan does just that.

Here are some examples of 'relief' activity with contrasting results:

- US missions teams who rushed to Honduras to help rebuild homes destroyed by Hurricane Mitch spent on average $30,000 per home – homes locals could have built themselves for $3,000 and which would have provided local employment opportunities.
- Consider, by contrast, the church that replaced its free 'clothing closet' with a thrift store that generated profits allowing it to employ former recipients and move them into productive jobs.

RELIEF

↓

REHABILITATION

↓

DEVELOPMENT

Phase II: REHABILITATION

In this phase, gospel-aligned sustainable habits for healthy living need to be taught. This includes encouraging healthy attitudes towards relationships, material goods, the world, and self. Sometimes this context is presented at first contact. For example, someone who asks you to help them with their debt is fundamentally asking you to teach them how to best manage their money, rather than for a fiver from your wallet!

At other times, you'll need to work at bringing someone through to the rehabilitation stage, from the relief stage. For example, a hungry homeless person isn't asking you for advice on how to get a council flat. They are asking you for a cup of hot soup. They are saying, "Help!" However, as you develop a relationship with this person in the context of the relief relationship, you are increasingly creating the context in which to start to address the system in which they became homeless. Is the issue about addiction? Is it about broken relationship? Is it about lack of self worth? None of those things can be resolved by hot soup alone!
In this respect, we are given the context in which to start to shine a light on these issues and offer teaching, signposting and services that might bring healing.

A good example of rehabilitation activity is modelled by the debt counselling organisation, Christians Against Poverty, who help people to budget wisely in order to stay out of debt long term, rather than simply teaching them how to pay off their debt in the short term.

Phase III: DEVELOPMENT

In this phase, redeemed attitudes need to be turned into sustainable Godly behaviours. Clearly, relief and rehabilitation aren't prerequisites to Development, but within the framework of meeting social poverty, it is a logical direction in which to operate.

Development activities identify and release the potential found within the person in order to remove the shame, fear and isolation that come with poverty. To teach someone an employable skill, not only increases their chance of obtaining financial security, but also increases their chances of finding shalom in all their attitudes and relationships.

Development opportunities also include inviting and receiving people to church, as this is the place where they are most likely to encounter ultimate rehabilitation and redemption through Jesus. It is a logical strategy to invite people to church events, or host social action events at the church building in order to break down unhealthy stereotypes, and encourage churchgoing behaviour. Participation in church life also gives us the opportunity to form relationships outside of the context of the poverty in question, just as should be the case with any other brother or sister at Gateway.

At Gateway we put this into practice through initiatives like Oasis, our ministry to women who have been victims of domestic violence. In the first instance, these women need relief — they need to escape from the situations they are in and be given emergency accommodation. It is important that they do not stay stuck in this relief phase though, and quickly move on to rehabilitation and development.

Seeking to tackle poverty in this way means investing time, energy and emotion, as well as money, and is much more demanding than just handing over some cash and hoping the problem will go away. But it offers the potential for a much more effective and longterm solution. It means joining in Christ's kingdom work, and being truly compassionate.

> *For you know the grace of our Lord Jesus Christ, that though he was rich, yet for your sake he became poor, so that you by his poverty might become rich.*
>
> (2 Cor 8:9)

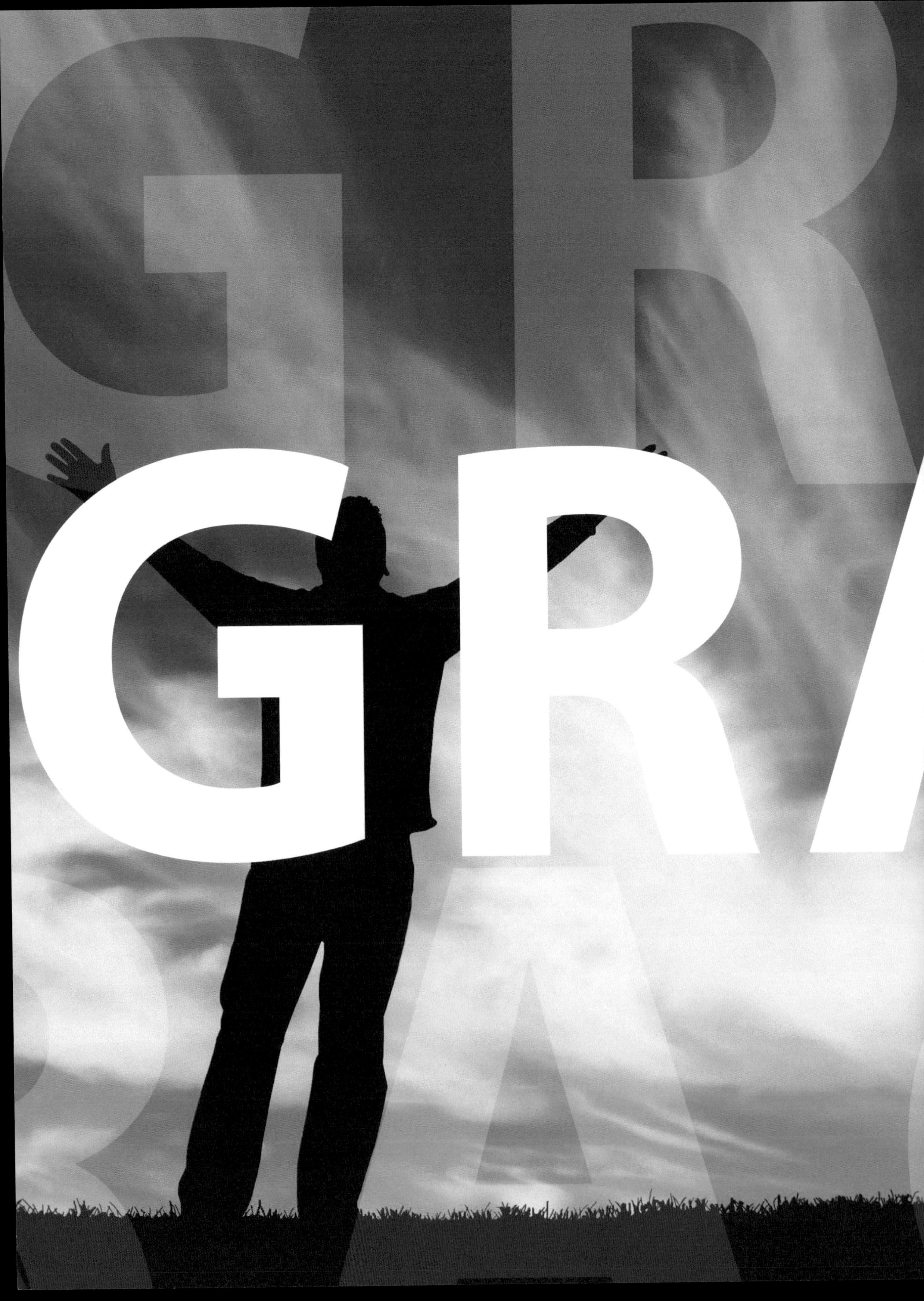
GR

ACE
of God

Commitment #4:
We are a people transformed by the grace of God

A church whose members understand and enjoy the grace of God is a fantastic place to be! There is joy, dynamism, confidence, and purity. You can feel it just as you can feel an atmosphere of legalism. Our church loathes legalism and adores the amazing grace of God!

God's grace is amazing because he saves us regardless of our background, status or gifting. God has given himself to us mercifully and bountifully in Christ. We don't deserve grace, but God lavishes it upon us.

When people think about having a relationship with God, often the first thought is, "I must obey". But cold obedience becomes legalistic, nothing more than following self-imposed rules and regulations. Instead, the Bible gives us a picture of a God who expects us to obey him, but to do so because we have experienced his grace at work in our lives. The main focus is not our weakness but God's grace.

This praise generating grace is also our guarantee of eternal security. God's grace to us is now and forever. It gives us great confidence! God is faithful. God is always reliable, always true to himself, and can be counted on to fulfil all of his promises.

If you are a believer it is because God has called you. And if he has called you, his grace is at work in you. You can therefore be thankful and confident, because God is a God of grace, and he will never let you go.

*"...we don't **deserve** grace, but God **lavishes** it upon us"*

Grace in the Bible

Grace is a hugely important word for Christians. It is a short word but its meaning is massive.

I love the fact that my wife is called Grace. This is a daily reminder to me of God's grace – I sleep with Grace and wake to Grace. My day is Grace-filled! But the thing about being married to Grace is that I mustn't merely be familiar with her – I need to really understand her. In the same way we need to really understand what God's grace means for us.

Grace is central in the Old Testament. As you read the Old Testament you will not often come across the word "grace" but the implications of grace are everywhere. God's grace is seen in his characteristics of being loving towards his people, showing them favour, and being merciful and compassionate towards them. These are all the outworking of grace. Whenever you read words like "love" or "mercy" or "favour" or "gracious" in the Old Testament you are reading about grace.

Psalm 86:15 describes the God of grace: *But you, O Lord, are a God merciful and gracious, slow to anger and abounding in steadfast love and faithfulness.* This is who God is!

When we move from the Old Testament to the New, suddenly the word "grace" begins to appear much more often. This word carries all the meaning of what is described about God in the Old Testament, but now assumes new and precious meaning because of the grace that is ours in Christ.

In this fuller description of grace, we see that grace is so much more than merely avoiding the punishment of God which we deserve. Grace is the means by which God actively saves us. Grace is the means by which God will for all time display through us his glory. Grace is God's free, unconditional gift to us.

In the letters of the New Testament the Apostles normally greet the churches with, "Grace to you." This greeting carries a sense of their history as Jews, a people who had been sustained by God's grace through the centuries. But is also has a new force, the force of men who have experienced God's amazing grace in Jesus.

May there be much grace to you, too!

Keeping grace front and centre

Grasping what grace means begins and ends with seeing:

1. Our need of salvation.
2. The impossibility of us saving ourselves.
3. The ability and goodness of God in saving us.

The normal human approach to religion is some version of seeking to live with a good conscience. We set a bar of behaviour and try to keep on the right side of it. This might seem to be a good thing, as it encourages people to live by certain standards and morals, but it is actually a disaster! Trusting in our own goodness sounds like good news but is in reality terrible news, because how can we ever know we are good enough? How do we know we have set the bar high enough?

By contrast, saying we need to trust in Jesus at first sounds like terrible news because it seems to remove human autonomy, self-effort, and so on. Actually it is the best news! It means the goodness I can rely on is not my own, but that of Christ. In Christ, there is no question of 'is it good enough?' because Christ is himself the one who sets the bar!

Moreover, rather than the goodness of Jesus condemning me, it saves me. It is not a case of, 'I can't match that standard, so am condemned by it', but 'his standard is now counted as mine'. The perfection of Jesus, not my self-deceiving conscience, is my rescue. My salvation is not dependent on how I have done today, but on what he has eternally done. Understanding this brings us into freedom, joy and security. That's what grace does!

What grace achieves

Grace is the way into salvation
It is not where we were born or who we were born to that opens the way to salvation for us. Rather, it is all of God's grace! This means the gospel is radically inclusive, with people from every country and culture brought into relationship with God. Christianity is not a western religion, but an offer of God's grace to all the peoples of the world.

Salvation is not dependent on the things we do
This is very good news because if salvation did depend on us we would always end up in insecurity, moralism or hypocrisy. We don't have to try and put on a spiritual façade, trying to convince ourselves, others, or God, that we are worthy of salvation. Instead we simply trust in Jesus! Salvation is a free gift and this frees us to live generously in return. Grace is amazingly liberating!

Grace gives us security

Ephesians 2:6 describes how Christians have been raised up with Christ and seated with him in the heavenly places. This means that while we are still very much in this world, with all of its joys, struggle and pain, we are already in a place of absolute security with Christ. Whatever happens to us, our place with Christ is secure, and this makes God's grace very precious in moments of crisis.

Grace produces an ongoing response to God

Hebrews 7:25 tells us that Jesus, *is able to save to the uttermost those who draw near to God through him, since he always lives to make intercession for them.* This describes a dynamic, ongoing relationship, rather than something that is static. Jesus does save us, once and for all, but we are to work out this salvation, knowing that Jesus is continually representing us before his Father.

Grace enables us to do good works, pleasing to God

Ephesians 2:10 says that, *We are his workmanship, created in Christ Jesus for good works, which God prepared beforehand, that we should walk in them.* Receiving the grace of God is not something we earn from good works, but we are called to do good works as an overflow of God's grace at work in us. Good works are a consequence, not a precondition, of God's grace. These works have been planned by God, for our good and for His glory. They are the things we do in order to witness to the grace that is at work in us.

Ephesians 2:6

"...and raised us up with him and seated us with him in the heavenly places in Christ Jesus"

a people who **joyfully** recognise the

SOVER

EIGNTY

of God

Commitment #5:
We are a people who joyfully recognize the sovereignty of God

God's sovereignty in our conversion: Called by God

All of us are called something and what we are called helps define who we are. If you had lived in Corinth two thousand years ago and been called "slave" you might have found it difficult to think like a free person. On the other hand, if you were used to being called "master" you might have found it difficult to start to act in a Christ-like, serving way. What Paul says to the Corinthians (and all Christians) is, *God, **who has called you** into fellowship with his Son Jesus Christ our Lord, is faithful.* (1 Corinthians 1:9)

It is God who has called you! And we have been called into fellowship – relationship – with Jesus. If we understand that God calls us and what it is he calls us to, the way we think and act will be transformed. When God calls us it is a summons of the King! God's call to us is made up of at least three distinct parts:

The facts
All have sinned and fall short of the glory of God (Romans 3:23)
The wages of sin is death (Romans 6:23)
While we were still sinners, Christ died for us (Romans 5:8)

An invitation to respond to Jesus in faith and repentance
Come to me, all you who are weary and burdened, and I will give you rest. Take my yoke upon you and learn from me, for I am gentle and humble in heart, and you will find rest for your souls. For my yoke is easy and my burden is light (Matthew 11:28-30).

Repent and be baptised, every one of you, in the name of Jesus Christ for the forgiveness of your sins (Acts 2:38).

A promise of forgiveness and eternal life
For God so loved the world that he gave his one and only Son, that whoever believes in him shall not perish but have eternal life (John 3:16).

When we respond to God's call, it is not something that we do simply by our own will and choosing. It is the grace of God that enables us to respond to his call. In fact, we could not respond to God unless he gave us the grace to do so. Our salvation is totally a work of God. This is what Jesus called being "born again" (see John 1:13, 1 Peter 1:3).

God's sovereignty in our conversion: Given new life by God

Without God's gracious, sovereign, intervention on our lives we would be utterly lost. As the apostle Paul expresses it, without Christ, *You were dead in your transgressions and sins* (Ephesians 2:1).

Things that are dead don't spontaneously come to life. Only God can cause new life to well up within us. When we are born again it as though the light comes on. Suddenly we see and understand things that previously were hidden to us. God breathes new life into us, and we are then made able to believe. But while our salvation is completely dependent on God doing his work in us, we still have to respond to God's work. This is what we call conversion, when in faith and repentance we turn to Jesus.

Knowing about Jesus is not sufficient for conversion. Faith equals trust. This trust is not simply belief *about* Jesus but belief *in* him. True conversion involves our whole being: we understand the truth intellectually, we approve of Jesus' claims emotionally, and we make a decision of the will to put our trust in him. There cannot be genuine faith without genuine repentance. We cannot accept Christ as Saviour but not as Lord. Repentance and faith are the two sides of the same coin, and they are both God's grace to us.

Our salvation is all the result of God's grace to us. God calls us and gives us new life. We respond by turning to Jesus in faith and repentance. And then God justifies us – he declares that we are forgiven and righteous. Being justified means we can say, ***its just as if I'd never sinned***. Rather than looking upon us as sinners deserving of punishment, God sees us as righteous. Grace teaches us that none of us deserve to be accepted by God, but that God in his grace will accept us regardless of what we do. And grace teaches us that we do not have to do anything to earn God's acceptance – he simply chooses to accept us.

Justification comes to us once we express faith in Jesus: *Therefore, since we have been justified through faith, we have peace with God through our Lord Jesus Christ* (Romans 5:1). When God says we are justified there is nothing else we can or should do to earn his acceptance. The Bible describes a great exchange. Jesus took our sin upon himself on the cross and now has clothed us in his righteousness. When we are justified we have peace with God!

God's sovereignty in our conversion: Declared to be God's children

When we become Christians God not only justifies us but he adopts us as his children – we become part of his family. People often say that "we are all God's children." Although this is true in a sense, it is not biblical theology! It is true that all humans are made in the image of God, but until our conversion we are far from being his children: *We all once lived in the passions of our flesh, carrying out the desires of the body and the mind, and were by nature children of wrath, like the rest of mankind* (Ephesians 2:3). Before we are Christians we are not God's children, we are children of wrath! We are enemies of God. But when we become Christians God adopts us as his own: *To all who received him, to those who believed in his name, he gave the right to become children of God* (John 1:12).

This is true of all Christians, without exception. We are all in the same family! The grace of God shown to us in adoption gives us a wonderful freedom and confidence – we are God's heirs, with all the rights and privileges that implies. While we are God's sons now, there is more to come. When Jesus comes again we shall receive our resurrection bodies which will be like his resurrection body. This is a great hope and promise. Imagine what it will be like to have a resurrection body! No more tiredness or illness. No more growing old and weak. Like a child receiving its inheritance we will receive the full measure of God's inheritance for us.

God didn't have to adopt us. He could have saved us without adopting us. He could have made us like the angels who clearly have right standing before God but do not share the privileges of family membership in the way we do. This is God's grace to us. We have an inheritance better than the angels!

Being adopted by God gives us all kinds of benefits and privileges. We can speak to God and relate to him as a good and loving Father. We can be confident that he does indeed love us. We can be confident that God understands us and cares for us. We know that as a good Father, God will give us good things. And when God adopts us we are suddenly surrounded by brothers and sisters in Christ. This is why the normal New Testament means of address is "brothers", meaning "brothers and sisters in the Lord". We are family together, and together share joy and pain. Whatever we go through, we are not alone.

God's sovereignty over all things: Why we are 'Reformed'

We believe that God is working out his purpose in the world, the church and our individual lives. We recognize that God is the prime mover in history and in our salvation and in this see ourselves belonging to the Reformed theological tradition. This is a huge subject, but here is a brief overview of how this plays out…

God's sovereignty and the world

All kinds of things happen to us which seem to be beyond our control. Sometimes these things are huge, while at other times they are trivial. For example, while I was preparing this the power suddenly went off in my house. I did what you are meant to do if the power goes off – first I checked the fuse box, which was fine, and I then checked the electiricty meter, which showed no power was coming into the house. So then I contacted the electricity supplier and asked them to sort it out.

When something like this happens we tend to ask the obvious questions: Why is it happening? Who is responsible? When will it be fixed? When the electricity guys had come along and dug a big hole in the street outside my house they concluded that the power cable had been bent by BT laying other cables and this had resulted in the cable eventually burning out, and my electricity supply being cut off. In this case, God was sovereign, but BT were responsible!

Ultimately Christ is sovereign, as is made clear in Colossians 1:16-17: *By him all things were created…in him all things hold together.* This means that the cables, the substation, the power station, the atoms and particles themselves – all of it was created by him, and holds together because of him.

God sovereign over all the affairs of men. Isaiah 40:15 says, *Behold, the nations are like a drop from a bucket, and are accounted as the dust on the scales; behold he takes up the coastlands like fine dust.* The great events of world history are to God just dust in a bucket.

This is a huge claim and one that is offensive to our sense of our own importance, but it is true! Much of the time we do not see this as obvious; it is no more obvious than the current running through the cable under the road and into my house, but it is just as real. One day God's sovereign rule will be made obvious, when all things are united in Christ (Eph 1:10), and this gives us confidence in a chaotic world. Whatever happens – *whatever happens!* – God is sovereign.

God's sovereignty and the church

God's saving of us is personal, but it is always worked out corporately. This is made very clear in the first chapter of Ephesians: *He blessed **us**…chose **us**…that **we** should be holy…he predestined **us**…**we** have redemption…* God's adoption of us is adoption into a family, not into solitariness.

Christ's saving work is for the church, because it is *through the church his manifold wisdom might be made known* (Eph 3:10). This means that the church is going to be ok! There have been many premature predictions of the church's imminent demise and the church has exprienced many hardships and setbacks, but Christ is building his church. This is a family to be optimistic about – it is not going to fold up and die, or be extinguished. The church will prevail because God is sovereign over it.

God's sovereignty and us

One time I jumped into the sea for a swim forgetting my car key was in my pocket. Of course, after that, the key wouldn't work and I had to run home to get the spare. Who was responsible? Me! Who was sovereign? God!

That God is sovereign does not diminish our personal responsibility. Equally, that we are responsible does not diminish God's sovereignty. What I do won't knock God off course; but it does matter. And when I am knocked off course it matters; but God is still sovereign.

We tend to think 'things going well' means 'God is in control', and 'things going badly' means 'God isn't in control', but truly recognizing God's sovereignty means recognizing it in all circumstances. This is why we have been given the book of Job! When Job loses all he possesses his response is, *Shall we receive good from God, and shall we not receive evil?* (Job 2:10). It is in the evil day that the rubber of faith hits the road of experience.

Bad things happen to us for any number of reasons. Sometimes it is because of our folly, when we do silly things, like jumping into the sea with our car keys. Sometimes it is because of our sin, when we tend to reap what we sow. Sometimes it is because we live in a fallen world – a world of haemorrhoids, hurricances and heart attacks.

In times of disaster God's sovereignty is either the live rail that will kill us or the anchor of hope that will save us. Job chose to grasp the anchor and was saved rather than "curse God and die" (Job 2:9). As those who have been made alive in Christ (Eph 2:5) and are guaranteed possession of a great inheritance (Eph 1:14) we should do likewise.

God's sovereignty and God

Many of the questions we have about the sovereignty of God are resolved when we look to the cross. At the cross we see human responsibility given full rein, and failing dramatically. Yet even in the midst of this human failing we see the Father's great sovereign plan being worked out. The cross was the darkest of times, but also the greatest of times, as it is because of the cross that we receive grace, forgiveness and a great inheritance. God is sovereign – believing and experiencing this brings us into peace and joy.

a people **committed** to
GENER

OSITY

Commitment #6:
We are a people committed to generosity

Setting the scene

Churches often have a bad reputation when it comes to money, and rightly so. Sometimes this is because churches present an impression of poverty, with tatty painted thermometers outside their buildings showing how much money has been raised for a new church roof from jumble sales and sponsored walks. Sometimes the problem is the other way around, with visions of TV evangelists in white suits asking for more money so they can buy another Mercedes. Even more seriously, at times churches fail in their mission because the people of God fail to give faithfully. And in some churches money is never mentioned because it is "private" – which reflects an attitude that is just embarrassing.

At Gateway we want to avoid all these kinds of financial pitfalls. We want to live generous lives, as good stewards of all that God has given us. We want the church to be supplied with all that it needs financially so that the mission is advanced, the staff well provided for, and the buildings maintained to a God-glorifying standard.

We want to be free from money controlling us and to be very free in using money to build the church. We want to be a people who respond to the generosity of God's grace in our lives by being lavishly generous in our giving. We want to demonstrate faith by aiming for daunting targets and trusting God to supply all our needs. We want to care for the poor, and to see the indebted walking free of their debts.

We want the church to be a place where money is handled right. And that starts with you!

How we should give

Material possessions often assume great importance for us but they also surprisingly often have little long term importance. Most of us have cupboards in our houses full of stuff that once seemed vital, but which we now never use. At Christmas many people get hugely stressed about buying lavish presents, but how many of us can remember what gifts we received last Christmas, let alone Christmas five years ago? As good stewards our focus should be less upon collecting ever more material possessions and more upon being generous. So, how should we give?

As an act of worship
Giving is not charity, or taxation. Giving to the work of the church is an act of worship. That is why it is good even if you give by Standing Order to sometimes give extra by cash or cheque on a Sunday. When the money just comes out of our bank accounts we can lose the sense of worship in giving, so it is good to physically give our money sometimes.

Without conditions
As giving is an act of worship it is important that we give without conditions. At Gateway we take our legal and charitable responsibilities seriously, with robust governance and financial procedures. However, when it comes to our giving, what the money is then used for is actually of less significance than the attitude with which we give. The act of giving is primarily an act of worship of God – in that sense it is a sacrifice, one that we trust God will delight in.

With regularity

If we do not give regularly we are less likely to give fully. If we think we will wait six months before giving it is likely that we will spend some of the money rather than keeping enough aside to give the full amount. If you receive a regular income it is wise to plan your giving to coincide with when you get the money. That is why it is good to give by Standing Order. That way you know your giving will be given!

In keeping with our income

Tithing, though a good principle, should not constrain our giving. Many of us can afford to give more than the tithe and many of us need to develop faith that comes from trusting God with more than the tithe. There is a challenge for us to keep our expenditure level while increasing our giving. We mustn't settle for merely tithing year after year and thinking we are doing well when actually our income means we could be giving much more. The more we earn the more we should give – "in keeping with his income."

Giving = Life

Our giving is about real, meaningful relationships. Our giving to this church is about life. Our giving is necessary to keep Gateway going! And our giving to others outside Gateway is about life – physical and spiritual.

We do teach tithing!

Tithing is something we believe in but understand many people have questions about. Tithing (giving away ten percent of income) has often been a controversial area for Christians. It has certainly at times been enforced in a way that does not reflect our understanding of the grace of God, and at other times been followed in a legalistic manner which again does not reflect our understanding of grace. At the same time, if every Christian tithed no church would be short of money! Even more important than 'raising funds' though, is what tithing achieves for us spiritually.

Here I want to set out ten reasons why I tithe, which might help you in the area of giving.

1 I follow the principle of the tithe because it teaches me to carefully manage my finances rather than estimate them.

If we are to give a tenth of our income we need to calculate what a tenth is! This is not legalism but accuracy, and helps with the overall management of our finances. We do not consider it legalism when our employer accurately calculates our salary and would be unhappy if he simply guessed what to pay us each month! In the same way we should be accurate in our giving.

2 I follow the principle of the tithe because it demonstrates gratitude and proves grace more powerful than law.

Tithing is not bringing in the Law. Abraham was justified when there was no law of Moses to guide him and he tithed when there was no law to enforce it! In Genesis 14:20 we read that Abraham tithed to Melchizedek the priest as an act of worship to God. Abraham's tithing was a response of gratitude for God rescuing him, and resulted in further blessing coming to him. The Israelites were commanded to tithe by Moses but Jesus never overturned this command, rather he endorsed it (Matthew 23:23).

When we tithe we are being obedient to the example of scripture, exercising faith and demonstrating our gratitude to the God who has saved us. Like Abraham, we are free from the law – we live in the age of the inner motivation of grace, but wouldn't it be a slap in the face for grace to come in lower than 10% and thus prove law to be more effective than grace? A true understanding of grace will move us to radical generosity.

3 I follow the principle of the tithe because it helps keep me consistent and disciplined.

John Piper says that *'another name for serious intention is planning… failure to plan …results not in spontaneity, but the same old rut'*. Again, we must not mistake discipline for legalism. The Bible instructs us to give cheerfully (2 Corinthians 9:7) and sometimes people twist this to mean we should only give when we feel like it. This is not the case! The Bible also instructs husbands to love their wives – whether or not they feel like it – and commands us to pray – whether or not we feel like it. When we do things we should do even though we don't feel like doing them we demonstrate our love for God and his priority in our lives.

4 I follow the principle of the tithe because it is proportional

No matter how much I earn, tithing keeps pace because it is a matter of proportion not amount.

5 I follow the principle of the tithe because it means giving the first 10%… and that is a demonstration of faith!

One of the key things about the law of the tithe in the Old Testament was that it was not giving any old 10%, but rather the *first* 10% of your income. This is the radical thing about the principle of the tithe. Giving the first tenth is a clear and powerful statement that you are putting God first – he is the first 'bill' you pay each month. Money talks. Think about it: you have no idea that you will come out okay that month. Unexpected bills might arrive that you could have used that 10% to pay. It is a statement of faith and trust in God to provide for you.

6 I follow the principle of the tithe to stay free from the love of money.

I have found that consistently surrendering a decent portion of my income (10% plus) to God on a monthly basis is an act of faith, obedience and worship that stops me worshipping money. Grace and I have always made our tithe and offerings the first item on our monthly budget, and we pay it before any other bill. This is because we are giving in faith, acknowledging that God comes first in our lives. We know that if we seek God first, he will always provide for us. We love God more than we love money.

7 I follow the principle of the tithe because I soon get used to it and don't 'miss' the money.

Once you are into the habit of tithing, then you get so used to living off 90% that you hardly even feel the hit. So, to keep on the faith stretch, Grace and I always give more than just 10% each month. Remember, 10% is not a law, although it might be a good target for you early on, but before long you will want to outstrip it. We are not trying to find the minimum that we can get away with, rather how much we can get away with!

8 I follow the principle of the tithe because it sets the example for all members of our church.

While the tithe is no longer a law for any of us, we recommend it as an appropriate amount for all members to give to the church each month. We want to be a church that is overflowing with the grace of God, and that must include excelling in the grace of giving (2 Corinthians 8:7).

9 I follow the principle of the tithe in order to invest in the future.

"Do not lay up for yourselves treasures on earth, where moth and rust destroy and where thieves break in and steal, but lay up for yourselves treasures in heaven, where neither moth nor rust destroys and where thieves do not break in and steal." (Matthew 6:19-20).

"As for the rich in this present age, charge them not to be haughty, nor to set their hopes on the uncertainty of riches, but on God, who richly provides us with everything to enjoy. They are to do good, to be rich in good works, to be generous and ready to share, thus storing up treasure for themselves as a good foundation for the future, so that they may take hold of that which is truly life."

(1 Timothy 6:17-19).

How interesting: God has no problem with us 'hoarding' up treasure for ourselves…so long as it is in the right place – in heaven not on earth.

10 I follow the principle of the tithe from a place of contentment.

Keep your life free from love of money, and be content with what you have, for he has said, "I will never leave you nor forsake you." So we can confidently say, "The Lord is my helper; I will not fear; what can man do to me?" (Hebrews 13:5-6).

Now there is great gain in godliness with contentment (1 Timothy 6:6).

The world system works to make us discontent with what we have so that we are always seeking more. In contrast to this, God urges us to get content with what we have and not be continually running after more and more.

Generosity in all of life

As well as generous giving as part of our worship, we want Gateway to be a church characterised by generosity in all we do. Christians should be the first to offer to buy the drinks, should give the largest tips and should have the most open homes. All that we have we have been given by God and we are meant to use all we have to glorify God. God is very generous, and when we are generous too we reflect and honour him.

a people who are committed to

GROW

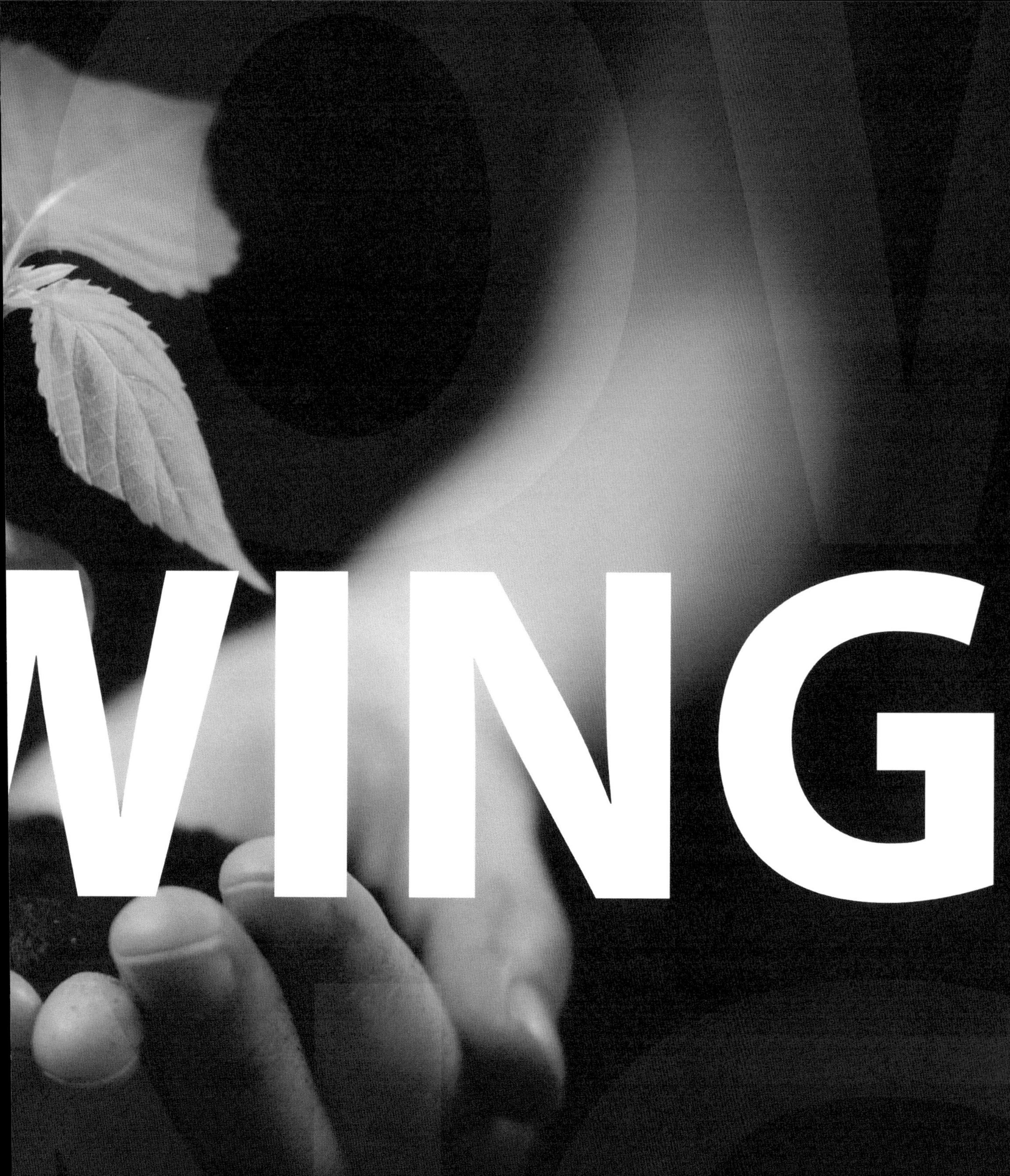
WING

Commitment #7:
We are committed to growing

Healthy things grow

In my garage there is a piece of wood on which I regularly mark the height of my children. It is amazing to see how they grow! Usually this growth is imperceptible – it just happens unnoticed – but when I stand them against that piece of wood and compare their height with where it was the year before the difference is incredible. Similarly, If we are healthy Christians we will grow. If Gateway is a healthy church it will grow. Simple as that!

Growth for followers of Jesus and for a church takes different forms, but we are looking for growth in *Quality* and in *Quantity*.

We want individual Christians to grow in their Christ-likeness. We want to become increasingly like Jesus and to live in a way which brings increasing honour to him. We also want believers to grow in what they understand and know.

We want our church to grow in quality and quantity. We want the sermons to be increasingly powerful, the worship band to be increasingly proficient, our prayer meetings to be increasingly fervent, our discipleship to be increasingly effective. We also want an increase in those things it is easier to measure – more guests, more baptisms, more people attending, more money given.

Wherever we decide to stop growing we are effectively deciding to die. Although I am no longer growing physically taller I want to keep growing in knowledge, love and godliness. I want to keep growing in my attitude. I want to keep growing in my relationships. If I stop working on these things I stop growing, and begin to die.

There are many things that will help you grow as a Christian and enable Gateway to grow as well – both numerically and in our devotion to Jesus. Chief among these is the Bible.

Growing in the word

We believe that the Scriptures of the Old and New Testaments in their original writing are fully inspired by God and accept them as the supreme and final authority for faith and life. In addition to being birthed through a powerful experience of the Holy Sprit, the church was also born into a devotion to the word of God. Not only are we passionate and intentional in pursuing the things of the Spirit, but we are equally devoted to sound theology and doctrine. Philip's first question to the Ethiopian was not, "Do you feel it?" but, "Do you understand?" (Acts 9:30)

So fundamental was the spread of the Word in the New Testament church that Luke described the growth of the church in these terms: *The word of God spread (Acts 6:7); The word of the Lord continued to increase and spread* (Acts 12:24); *The word of the Lord spread widely and grew in power* (Acts 19:20). Luke could have said that the churches multiplied, or that the number of disciples grew, but on these occasions, he spoke about the ever-increasing impact of the **word** of God.

Even after his resurrection, fully equipped with a body that could appear and disappear at will, Jesus did not overwhelm his disciples with supernatural tricks, but, opening the Scriptures, *explained to them what was said in all the Scriptures concerning Himself* (Luke 24:27). This was consistent with his earlier ministry in which we read, *Jesus saw a large crowd and had compassion on them, because they were like sheep without a shepherd. So he began teaching them many things* (Mark 6:34).

The preaching of God's Word is a very important ingredient in our Sunday meetings, and we usually set aside at least thirty-five minutes for preaching from the Bible.

Read to grow!

Every believer should have a planned method of reading the Bible

Over the course of time we should be reading all through the Bible. If you don't have a Bible reading plan the reality is that your Bible reading will be something like this… First, you will tend to read the Bible irregularly; chances are you'll find that a day or two, or a week or two, or a month or two, go by without you having read your Bible at all. And then you'll find that if you do read your Bible you will tend always to turn back to the same bits – those that you particularly like, or are familiar with or that you find easy to understand.

What is the problem with this?! Well, the problem is that you miss out on so much of the counsel of God and you are not taking personal responsibility for your spiritual health.

What stops us from reading the Bible?

One of the things that can hinder us from planning how to read the Bible is that we tend to think that only spontaneous things are good. *For those things which are essential to life it is far more liberating to have regularity and planning than spontaneity.* I find it is much more healthy to eat breakfast, lunch and dinner every day, rather than some days having six meals and the next day having none. And when it comes to the word of God I find it is far healthier to be planned than to wait for the spontaneous moment when I suddenly feel inspired to sit down and read Numbers!

I find it amazing the excuses people make for not reading the Bible! These normally boil down to just two excuses, 1. I'm too busy; or, 2. I don't like reading. And sometimes, "I'm too busy *and I* don't like reading!"

Saying this would be fine if the Bible were just another book. But it is far more than just writing – it is God's means of life to us. If we don't want to trip on the path of life we need the light of God's word to guide us.

If you don't like reading or are not very good at reading it is understandable why you find it difficult to get into the Bible. It is a very long book, and it has some difficult things in it, and some parts of it are, to be honest, rather dull, unless God illuminates them for us. But the reality is that *I have never met anyone who cannot give focussed attention to the things that really matter to them* – whether it is car maintenance, or playing video games, or keeping up with the football scores, or watching their favourite TV show. If the motivation is there you will overcome whatever obstacles stand in your way to achieve the thing you want to achieve.

Here are some tips to help you get into the word

- If you struggle to read or have a long commute get an audio bible downloaded onto your MP3 player
- Alternate between Old and New Testaments
- Keep a record of what you have read
- Read to receive, not simply to tick off a list
- Don't feel guilty if you miss your bible reading – feel thirsty!

"Saying this would be fine if the Bible were just another book. But it is far more than just writing – it is God's means of life to us. If we don't want to trip on the path of life we need the light of God's word to guide us."

Growing in prayer and worship

Jesus exclaimed to the Pharisees, *My house will be called a house of prayer* (Matthew 21:13). We want our church to be known as a praying church. Prayer demonstrates that we do not build the church by our might or power, but by the Spirit of God. Prayer releases the power of God.

We regularly give over time in to praying out loud together. If you are not used to this way of praying it can be a little off-putting at first, but very soon you will begin to enjoy the sense of unity and power that comes from everyone raising their requests to God together.

Both the Old and New Testaments paint a picture of very *lively* and *joyful* church meetings! The Bible mentions that *singing, clapping, dancing* and *shouting* are appropriate expressions of our worship to God. We want people in our meetings to feel very free in their worship of God.

The Bible also makes it clear that church meetings should be characterised not just by preaching and singing, but by the use of spiritual gifts. When we are gathered in God's presence we expect to know God's power! As well as this type of contribution it is vital that all of us learn how to participate in prayer and worship. *Contribution* is when one person bringing something to the meeting; *Participation* is when every part of the body plays their part. Not everyone can contribute at every meeting, but we can all participate!

Sometimes we can fail to participate because we feel we do not know quite what to do while everyone else does. It can be like dancing – we want to look like we know what we are doing but secretly are afraid of falling over our feet! This can lead to a terrible passivity in meetings. Sometimes it means that people don't come to prayer meetings, or feel very uncomfortable in them when they do. Don't be passive! God loves to hear enthusiastic prayer and worship, so go for it!

Seven steps to help you grow in prayer and worship

1 Develop your own devotional life: If you want to be good at something you have to practice! Praying and worshiping with other believers is a vital part of the Christian life but we also need to be pray-ers and worshippers on our own as well as in the crowd.

2 Use the Bible: In meetings often a scripture will be shared which you can latch onto and use to focus your thoughts and words. Looking at your Bible is also the launch pad for contribution. If you stir your soul with inspiring scripture it is more likely that the Spirit of God will work through you to bring a word of exhortation, another language or prophecy or a great prayer to the meeting.

3 Come Prepared: While leadership is important, we should not be dependent on the worship leader, preacher, small group leader or prayer meeting leader. We all need to feel responsible for the meeting. We should come to meetings expecting to participate, not waiting for someone to make us participate! We must also remember who it is we are coming to – the Lord. He is worthy of our best.

4 Learn from those further on: We shouldn't be embarrassed about learning from those who are further on than us in their devotion to God. Get close to people who are passionate about God, and avoid those who are cynical or complaining.

5 Cast aside inhibition: Introverts do not have to become extroverts, but the gospel is about freedom and this includes the freedom to worship and pray without inhibition.

6 Be open to the Spirit: The Spirit prays and worships! Being open to the Spirit will give us assurance that God is "Abba, father." This kind of assurance is the chief antidote to inhibition. The Spirit also gives us spiritual gifts that bring us into freedom and he teaches us how to pray. The Spirit loves to glorify Jesus and if we are open to him he will enable us to glorify Jesus too.

7 Use your head: When we come to pray and worship we should not leave our brains behind. The renewing of our minds involves an increased ability to concentrate on spiritual things and we need to use our minds when we pray and worship.

Growing in mission

Too often the Church has the false assumption that it is primarily a pastoral community. This is wrong, although pastoring is an essential part of the church. The church presented in scripture is clearly a pioneering, apostolic movement, devoted to reaching the lost at any cost. This means that the local church is not primarily a pastoral community existing to meet one another's needs. Rather it is a pioneering community on a mission, and we'll meet each other's needs on the way. Pastors are called to lead the flock on the mission, and care for it along the way.

Our church is more concerned with winning people to Christ than it is about the comfort of its members. But, by the grace of God, a church with this attitude reaps abundant care, love and pastoring! An important part of your own spiritual growth will be an increasing desire to share the gospel with others. We are not a holy huddle – we are on a mission to win the lost!

As part of our desire to grow in pioneering we are committed to church planting and global mission. The first church in Jerusalem planted out many times. Church planting is not just for some churches, it is an indispensable biblical value for every church. Most people will not leave our church to start another church, but all of us are involved in this mission of church planting. Similarly, we want all members of Gateway to feel our shared responsibility to make disciples of all nations – whether or not we actually go to live in a different country.

Sizing the church

There is no one perfect size for a church. The reality is that all of us have a "size preference" with which we feel most comfortable. The trouble is that it is easy to make what is simply our preference into a matter of immovable doctrine! Many people have a size preference for a small church. This is because in a small church it is possible to know the names of everyone else in the congregation and to feel very comfortable about where you fit. In a larger church you will not know the names of everyone, or even the majority of people and it is possible to feel lost in the crowd. Other people prefer larger churches because there is typically more going on in these communities, with more resources and a greater sense of momentum.

The great danger of a small church preference is that it clamps a lid upon mission. **But:** A local church is not meant to exist for itself but to reach out to those outside the church! This means that healthy churches will always have lots of new people joining them. The danger of a larger church is that it is possible to become a passive consumer of church 'services' without any sense of having a contribution to make yourself.

Gateway is not going to be a church which exists for the comfort of its members but is a church where the members reach out to new people and seek to draw them to Christ and his church. The way we feel led to help solve some of the tensions that can exist between large and small, growing and pastoring, is to keep our Sunday meetings fairly small, but to grow the number of meetings and locations we have. This way we hope to enjoy the benefits of a larger church in terms of the things we have the resources to achieve, but also the benefits of a smaller church in terms of our connections with one another.

committed to

PASTO

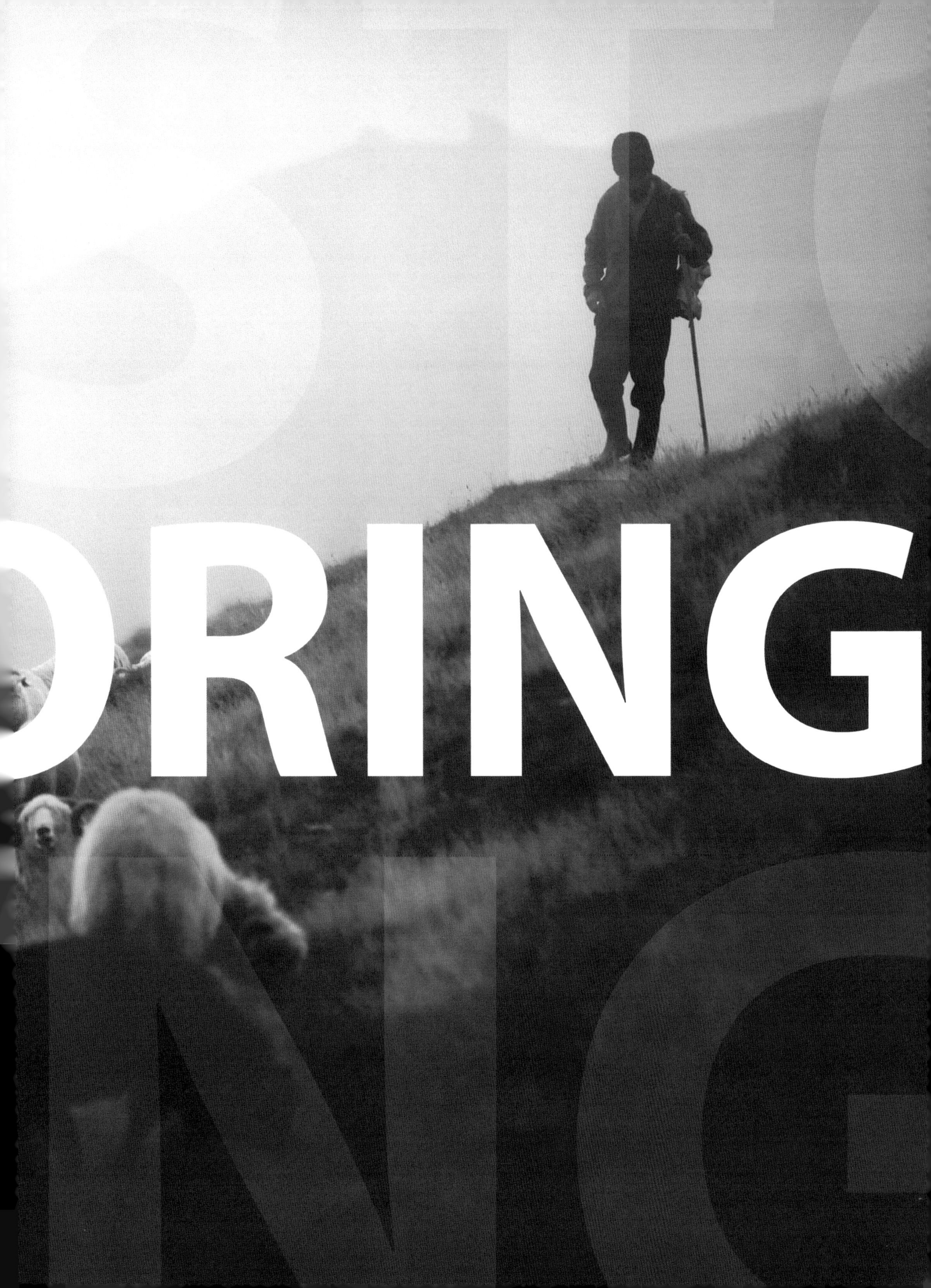
ORING

Commitment #8:
We are committed to pastoring

Understanding leadership in the church

While we believe strongly in the priesthood of all believers, we also believe that leadership is a gift from God and is to be exercised in the church. But, vitally, leadership is there to serve the people, and not the other way round.

Gateway is led by an elder team

"Elder" is a description of office, rather than seniority through age. In church life you don't move into increasing leadership responsibility with increasing age but by the anointing and appointing of God. Our elders are men who are recognized by the congregation, the other elders and the apostolic team who help us, as having spiritual authority to lead at Gateway. There are three broad areas for which the elders are responsible:

> **Guarding:** Because eldering is primarily about *being* rather than *doing,* elders must keep themselves in a good place with God. Elders must also guard the truth. This is because the word of God is sacred and must be protected, but also because both *truth and lies* are powerful. Wonky doctrine produces wonky lives. Sound doctrine produces sound lives. Elders also need to guard the flock from 'wolves'. These are people who bring danger to the flock such as false teachers, the sexually immoral, those who are negative and gossiping, and those causing division and strife.

> **Guiding:** Elders guide the church like shepherds. Elders are out-in-front as the primary vision-bearers and pace setters. They lead their church into the likeness of Christ, and on mission into neighbourhoods and nations.

> **Governing:** Governing means to direct the affairs of the church, which needs to be done diligently. Elders govern the church through: Preaching and teaching; the setting of vision and values; the setting of strategy; the appointment of leaders; thorough discipleship of the believers; performing church discipline when necessary.

Understanding spiritual authority

Leadership is a gift from God to his church and is to act with real authority. Where does this spiritual authority come from?

All authority resides in God

God is over all, sovereign, the creator and sustainer of all things. Because we respect and obey God we also submit to all authority he has instituted, *unless it clearly contradicts his revealed will.* This is why we teach the submission of citizens to government, pupils to teachers, employees to employers, wives to husbands and church members to elders.

Rebellion against God's authority is the root of all evil

Rebellion was the original sin, and God hates it! Satan loves a rebellious spirit and laughs when a rebellious person preaches the word, leads a church or other ministry. We are not to be rebels.

1 Peter 5:1-5

"So I exhort the elders among you, as a fellow elder and a witness of the sufferings of Christ...
...shepherd the flock of God that is among you, exercising oversight, not under compulsion, but willingly, as God would have you; not for shameful gain, but eagerly; [3] not domineering over those in your charge, but being examples to the flock...
...Likewise, you who are younger, be subject to the elders. Clothe yourselves, all of you, with humility toward one another, for "God opposes the proud but gives grace to the humble.""

God's kingdom is one of order
The church must accept God's authority and reflect his order if she is going to be effective.

Submission is absolute, obedience is relative
Submission is a matter of attitude while obedience is a matter of conduct. This means that when leaders act in a way that is clearly contrary to the revealed will of God we are free not to obey them yet we are to remain submissive.

To be given spiritual authority we need to come under authority
Whoever we are we need to find out who God wants over us in the Lord and be subject to them. Once we learn to come under authority we will find a secure, healthy place from which we can ourselves exercise authority. Rebellion ultimately disqualifies us and God will remove our authority.

Spiritual authority comes with God's ordaining not man's attaining
Once God's anointing and appointing is recognised we must be careful not to slander or speak against it. We must maintain the dignity of God's anointed leaders. A rebellious spirit delights in spotting defects in authorities and belittling them. This gives excuse for throwing off restraint. But this attitude – the spirit of our age – is judged by God.

Church membership is an invitation to be pastored

Jesus is the chief shepherd of the church who appoints under-shepherds (elders) to pastor local churches (1 Pet 5:1-5). Clarity about church membership is essential if the elders are to know who they are responsible for. This is not merely a matter of ticking things off administratively, but an important spiritual matter, as the under-shepherds will one day have to give account to the chief shepherd for those entrusted to their care (Heb 13:17).

Sometimes people say, "Why should I become a member of a particular church? I don't see any verses commanding this in the New Testament." This is a mistaken attitude!

God keeps lists of who His people are. The Old Testament is full of these lists, but the New Testament also makes it clear that God keeps a list of all believers (Philippians 4:3; Revelation 21:27).

We also see examples of church life in the New Testament that indicate the churches must have kept lists of who was in membership. Paul's instructions to *put out* a sinner at the church in Corinth (1 Corinthians 5) means there must have been a way of knowing who was *in*! We also know that the early church kept a list of widows (1 Timothy 5:9). If the churches kept such lists, it is reasonable to assume that they had a list of all church members.

Membership of a particular church is a normal part of being a Christian, and there are many reasons and benefits in this.

- It identifies you as a **genuine believer** (Ephesians 2:19, Romans 12:5). When you join a local church it signifies that the other members of that church recognise and endorse your salvation. This is important because church membership must be about a recognition of our shared faith in Jesus, and not simply signing up to a social club.
- It provides a **spiritual family** to support and encourage you in your walk with Christ (Galatians 6:1-2, Hebrews 10:24-25). Church membership signifies that you have a genuine love for God and His people.
- It gives you a place to **discover and use your gifts** in ministry (1 Corinthians 12:4-27). Church membership signifies that you will be united with these people in seeking to advance the gospel of Jesus Christ using the gifts God has given you.
- It places you under the **spiritual protection** of godly leaders (Hebrews 13:17, Acts 20:28-29). Church membership signifies that you are not a lone ranger, but prepared to be taught and cared for by those God has appointed to lead His church.
- It gives you the **accountability you need to grow** (Ephesians 5:21). Church membership signifies that you will be committed in attending, giving, praying and serving and that others will help you grow as a disciple of Jesus.

Added and devoted

A phrase frequently used in the New Testament to describe people's response to the gospel is that they *were added* to the church. They did not simply get right with God; they were *added* to the company of disciples. If we are to truly love and respect Jesus we must also be devoted to his church. Of course, no local church is ever perfect — and if you ever found a perfect church you would only make it imperfect by joining it! Every local church has its own strengths and weaknesses, reflecting the people who make it up. But this lack of perfection does not excuse us from devotion.

When we read the letters that the apostles wrote to the churches in the New Testament we very quickly see that none of them was perfect. But at no point did Paul or Peter or John say to Christians, "leave the church." Always the command was, "be devoted — and by the grace of God, Christ in his perfection will overcome your imperfections." The early Christians were devoted to fellowship. They wanted to work out their new life by a thoroughgoing expression of love and loyalty to one another and the work. With every member playing his or her part, no one person is overloaded, but the whole body functions well together.

Being a follower of Jesus is often tough. We face all kinds of temptations and opposition, from the world, the flesh and the devil. In order to remain faithful we need friends of like heart and mind. When we join a local community of believers we are united with others who have experienced the same grace of God in their lives. And we are plunged into relationships, with all the delights and challenges they bring!

Occasionally, and very sadly, it becomes necessary to exclude someone from church life because of ongoing unrepentance. *When people exclude themselves from discipleship, they exclude themselves from the church.* It is indeed staggering that some believers voluntarily choose to live in this state! Church discipline is when the gathered church ratifies this exclusion. The aim of exclusion is twofold: that the shock, or shame, of exclusion will cause the offender to repent and become a disciple again; and that the harmony and integrity of the church should not be compromised by pockets of rebellion. Over all this is the ultimate aim: to God be glory in the church!

The commitment of membership

The difference between just attending Gateway and becoming a member of Gateway is a little like the difference between being married to someone rather than just living with them. Both arrangements look similar, but marriage expresses a commitment that is lacking if a couple decide to just shack up together. Importantly, church membership is different from marriage because it is not a lifetime commitment. However, we do take membership seriously and ask members of Gateway Church to seek to:

- Grow in their experience of God's grace
- Grow in their knowledge of and love for Jesus
- Become increasingly committed to the body of Christ, as expressed at Gateway
- Become increasingly generous with their money and possessions
- Use their gifts to the glory of God to the fullest possible extent.

These things are worked out by church members:

Protecting the unity of the church
by acting in love toward other members,
by refusing to gossip and
by following the leaders.

Sharing the responsibility of the church
by praying for its growth,
by inviting the unchurched to attend and
by warmly welcoming those who visit.

Serving the ministry of the church
by discovering their gifts and talents,
by being equipped to serve by the leaders and
by developing a servant's heart.

Supporting the witness of the church
by attending faithfully,
by living a godly life and
by giving generously.

Making these commitments to Jesus, and one another, is a significant thing. It is the kind of radical step that identifies disciples!

committed to

TEA

Commitment #9:
We are committed to team

At Gateway we believe in team and in team ministry. The church is led by an elders team, and the 's' in elders is important! The pattern we see in the New Testament is of teams of elders appointed to lead local churches, rather than a solitary pastor, and this is the model we follow. Our elders team recongnises one anothers gifts and strengths and compensates for one anothers weaknesses. We have regular team meetings, we hold one another accountable, and we meet together regularly with our wives. We want to work together as an effective team in order to serve Gateway well and honour Jesus among us.

There is also a deacon team at Gateway. These men and women assist the elders in the pastoral care of the church and we meet together regularly for training, to pray for church members, and to plan our pastoral strategy. The elders and deacons together form the core of the 'wider team', which includes others with key leadership responsibility in the church, and there are numerous other teams (trustees, worship team, kids team, etc.) which serve and resource what we do together as a church. Every church member is a member of the team too, with a contribution to make and a role to play. Church membership means being signed up to the team!

Our commitment to team is not a contemporary invention, but reflects a consistent biblical theme. Team is not something dreamed up by 21st century management consultants but reflects God's intention as to how life is meant to be done.

For instance, in 2 Corinthians 2:12-13 we are given an amazing little insight into Paul's approach to team: *When I came to Troas to preach the gospel of Christ, even though a door was opened for me in the Lord, my spirit was not at rest because I did not find my brother Titus there. So I took leave of them and went on to Macedonia.* When we read Acts and the epistles it is clear that Paul always worked in team – his letters are peppered with references to his team and it is very clear that while he was enormously gifted Paul was never a solo flyer. The situation in 2 Corinthians is that Paul had heard troubling reports about the church in Corinth and his teammate Titus had gone to check things out. Paul had been travelling through Greece and Turkey and got to Troas on the Aegean shore. He was there to preach, and his preaching was making an impact, but he didn't stay in Troas. Why? Because he wanted to see Titus! Paul was committed to Titus, was committed to the Corinthians and committed to team!

The Bible and team

Team Trinity

God himself is committed to team because God is 'Team Trinity'. There is only one God, but the one God is three persons: Father, Son and Holy Spirit. In Team Trinity there is eternal joy and delight and the perfect outworking of God's perfect plan. For example, we see the Trinity working as a team in planning and enacting our salvation: the Father predestines us for adoption as sons; it was Jesus who came to earth, living among us and offering himself as the perfect sacrifice to reconcile us to God; and it is the Holy Spirit who fills and empowers us.

If God himself works in team, it follows that we are designed for team too. It is not merely an accident of evolution that human beings choose to cooperate with one another in pursuit of common objectives, but part of what it means to be made in the image of God.

Creation

In the creation account God makes Adam and a teeming earth full of animal life, but… *It is not good that the man should be alone; I will make him a helper fit for him* (Gen 2:18). God creates Eve to work alongside Adam – they are to be a team. That story tells us what marriage is meant to be like – that a married couple are called to work together and there are things they can only achieve together. The obvious outworking of team Adam and Eve is children. They were called to grow the team and they did this by having babies.

There is application for all of us in this biblical example, whether we are married or not. When God said, "It is not good for the man to be alone" he was making it clear that we are meant to be in family and team together. This is what the church is!

Throughout the rest of the Bible we see examples of team. Sometimes these examples of team are very positive, while at other times we are given warnings about what happens when teams do not function as they should. When God called Abram to be blessed and be a blessing to all nations it was the beginning of 'Team Israel'. In reality, this was often a dysfunctional team (if you think your family is bad, read Genesis!) but the goal of the team was clear, and God's plan was that it should be fulfilled.

Team Israel

In the story of Israel's wandering in the wilderness we see examples of team success. For example, when the people brought such extravagant offerings for the Tabernacle that they had to be restrained from bringing more (Ex 36:3-7). At other times we see examples of team failure, such as when spies were sent into the promised land (Numbers 13). This was a time for team! A team of twelve spies, representing the entire team, were meant to stir faith in the whole team to enter the land. But instead of sirring faith they siphoned it away. Teams stand or fall on their faith – at Gateway we want to be full of faith!

Once Team Israel was in the land and established they still needed team. We see this with king David, who despite his outstanding personal characteristics of being a great warrior, great leader, great strategist, and great man of God, still needed to surround himself with a team. (See the list of David's mighty men in 2 Sam 23:8-39)

Later in Israel's history we are given a beautiful picture of team when under the leadership of Nehemiah the people rebuil the walls of Jerusalem (Nehemiah 3). The whole team gets involved in the tasks, including those who were not natural builders, such as goldsmiths, perfumers, and a man with his daughters. In fact only 'the nobles who would not stoop' (v5) didn't participate. This is a salutatory lesson for us – teamwork takes some stooping! Proud people tend not to do well in team.

New Testament Teams

When we get to the New Testament we see the theme of team continuing. Jesus himself recruits a team, calling the twelve disciples to follow him. There was real variety in this team: fisherman, a tax collector, a freedom fighter. There would have been a cost in joining this team, because freedom fighters and tax collectors didn't normally hang out together, and it wasn't always a harmonious team – but it was a team used by Jesus to turn the world upside down.

And so we come to the apostle Paul, who wouldn't stay in Troas without his teammate Titus. What an insight into team!

Every team has a leader

As we look at the biblical examples of team it is clear that teams always have a leader, whether that is God the Father, Moses, David, Nehemiah, Jesus or Paul. This is a positive thing! Leadership is not something to be sceptical about, but to embrace. At Gateway, the elder team leads the team of the church, and the elder team is led by the team leader. This enables the team to function efficiently and to stay united in vision and purpose.

The team is bigger than the sum of its parts

There is a significant difference between team and dictatorship. In a dictatorship everything revolves around one person, but in a team there is the recognition that no one person can do it all. For example, in our elder team we are all very clear that none of us is the complete article. Instead, we recognize and complement one another's strengths and compensate for one another's weaknesses. As a team we are able to get much more done than we ever would on our own.

Every team member has a role to play

At Gateway being a member of the church means being on the team. Church members are not consumers, being spoon fed by the elders. No, every member has a responsibility to be involved in doing the stuff! We are God's adopted children, with all the rights and privileges of sons, called to be active in his house.

The team has a shared purpose

Team Trinity has a clear purpose – to rescue and redeem all of God's people. At Gateway we have shared purpose – all of the things that are set out in this course! We are part of Jesus' team, caught up in his purpose, and called to spread the fragrance of the knowledge of him everywhere (2 Cor 2:15).

This understanding of team is one of the reasons why we place a strong emphasis upon church membership. If you come into membership it is a clear statement that you want to be part of the team, and not merely an onlooker. It is much better to be in the thick of the action as a team member than a casual observer from the sidelines. Gateway is a great team – we hope you will join it!

*"As a **team** we are able to get **much more** done than we ever would on our **own**"*

committed to
COMM

Commitment #10:
We are committed to community

Keeping church simple

The two things we focus on most are doing our Sunday meeting well and doing our Life Groups well. We are convinced that if we can get these two things right we will effectively cover 90% of what needs to be done in church life.

Sunday morning is the "big meeting" in the Gateway week. It is the focal point for our life together – our most visible demonstration of community. We approach Sunday's with a real sense of purpose, expectant of God's presence and power with us as we gather to him.

We work hard at trying to break the mind-set which thinks of church *buildings* as being church, but because we are a people on a mission, we don't want to be hidden away in a corner. We want people to know that we are here! The Sunday meeting is our shop window, so we do everything we can to make people aware of it. Because our Sunday meetings are publicly visible, coming to them is a public declaration that you identify with what they represent. Our meetings are not just meetings! They are a prophetic statement of our being part of the Body of Christ, of being part of this community.

The New Testament gives us a model of the first church meeting in both large and small groups. The book of Acts paints a picture of the early church growing rapidly in numbers, but also meeting from house to house: *Every day they continued to meet together in the temple courts. They broke bread in their homes and ate together with glad and sincere hearts* (Acts 2:46). Whenever the apostle Paul went to a new area to spread the message of Jesus, he would use public buildings like synagogues or market places in which to preach, but he would also be based in a house and begin to gather a church there.

Two-winged church

A helpful image is to think of the church as having two wings. One wing is our large meetings and the other is our small groups. Without two wings a bird cannot fly. Our experience and the lessons of church history teach us that a one winged church will not fly either. Church needs to be experienced in the power of the congregation and in the relationships of the small group. And every one of us who together make up the church need to be part of the large and the small. We should not be one winged Christians or we will simply find ourselves flapping around in circles, unable to get off the ground!

At Gateway we call our small groups **Life Groups.**

Life Groups are not an optional extra – Life Groups are our priority. This means that by far the most important programme in the church is our Life Groups. How we structure our small groups changes from time to time (the structure of what we do is far less important than the doing of what we do!), but we have found that it is not possible to care effectively for someone who is not plugged into genuine fellowship by being part of a Life Group – it simply doesn't work. Those who only meet at the "temple" never know the joys and blessings of genuine New Testament church life. Having small groups does not guarantee a strong sense of community in the church, but without them creating community is exceptionally difficult!

There are five core values we build Life Groups around:

1 **Friendship:** The bigger Gateway gets the happier we will be! This is because we want as many people as possible to respond to the gospel of Jesus Christ and be added to His church. We like big crowds but know that the big crowd is not always the easiest place to make friends. We want every member of the church to be in a Life Group because we want every member of the church to have friends in the church.

2 **One-anothering:** Life Groups are the most important aspect of the pastoral care system in the church. If you are not in a Life Group it is going to be hard to care for you. We want to build community on a mission for Jesus. On this mission we must look out for one another Life Groups help us do this effectively.

3 **Outreach:** If there is one word we would use to sum up what the church is about it is this: "Mission!" Outreach has to be at the centre of our Life Groups because it is central to Jesus' plan for his church. He has commissioned us to *"Go! and make disciples of all nations."*

4 **Teaching:** When Jesus commissioned the disciples to "Go!" he told them to go "teaching" (Matthew 28:20). Teaching is a core activity of church life. At our Sunday services we devote a considerable part of the meeting to teaching, but this then needs to be applied and worked out in our lives. The best place for this application is in a Life Group, where there is the time and space to discuss the Word of God together, and help one another be true to it.

5 **Body Life:** Every believer is called to be a minister (2 Corinthians 5) and every believer is to be equipped to minister (Ephesians 4). Life Groups are the perfect place for us to do this. In a Life Group there should be an experience of spiritual gifts, of prayer, of worship. Life Group is where we get to practice our gifts, and where no-one minds if we are not an expert!

The Lord's Supper

When Jesus was about to finish his ministry on earth by going to the cross, he gathered his disciples and commanded them how they were to remember him once he had returned to his Father in heaven. The means of remembrance was to be in a meal, the Lord's Supper. The Lord's Supper should be the high point of our worship together because it is the moment at which we most visibly see the community of God and his people.

Why should we celebrate the Lord's Supper?
The purpose of the Supper is proclamation – proclaiming the death of Jesus. We *celebrate* and *proclaim* Jesus' death because it is his death that has bought us salvation. So the Supper is to be taken repeatedly as a repeated reminder of what Jesus' death has accomplished for us.

This proclamation is repeated but temporary. It is only "until he comes." So taking the Supper reminds us of the certainty of Jesus' return. Christ's death is not the end but the beginning of the end – there is a future for all the people of God.

Food and celebration go hand in hand. We would never have a birthday party or wedding without food. When we take bread and wine in the Lord's Supper we celebrate what Jesus has done for us. We celebrate looking forward to the greatest celebration of all, "the wedding feast of the lamb" (Revelation 19:9). And we celebrate because we are gathering to Jesus – we are coming into his presence. This means communion should not be mournful or introspective, but joyful!

We proclaim Christ's death in terms of victory and not in a morbid reflection on the sufferings of Christ. The New Testament never dwells on the sufferings of Christ; instead it celebrates the achievements of the cross. The word 'proclaim' has the ring of victory not defeat about it, and this is how we should celebrate the Lord's Supper. We participate in the Supper as a sign of what we have become: participators in Christ, one loaf, one body.

Communion is not some strange religious rite that is out of keeping with contemporary culture. It is a powerful proclamation – of what has been done, what will be done and of who we are.

The Lord's Supper is a meal

The first Lord's Supper took place at the time of the Jewish Passover. Whereas at the Passover a lamb was sacrificed, now Jesus was going to be sacrificed. Whereas at the Passover the liberation of Israel was celebrated, now the liberation of all the earth was to be celebrated. Just as the Passover was eaten in a home, so the early Christians would have eaten the Lord's Supper in a home. At the Passover the head of the house would break bread at the beginning of the meal and proclaim what God had done; he would later pass round wine and again proclaim God's deliverance. Jesus followed this pattern in the Lord's Supper and so did the early churches.

We regularly celebrate the Lord's Supper in our Sunday meetings. Communion in this setting cannot normally take the form of a proper meal and inevitably has to have a certain formality about it in order that the bread and wine can be distributed "with decency and order." Exactly how we celebrate the Supper in this setting will vary from time to time but every time we want there to be celebration and proclamation! This means that communion should normally be loud rather than quiet! Taking the Supper together in the gathered congregation is a powerful declaration of what we believe and whom we have come to worship.

We also encourage our Life Groups to regularly celebrate the Supper. In a small group we can have a proper meal together, during the course of which we boldly declare and proclaim what Jesus has done.

Eating together demonstrates unity

When we eat a meal with someone it is a sign of acceptance of them. In the Passover meal everyone in the household ate the meal together, demonstrating how each of them had been rescued by God. The Lord's Supper was similarly intended to demonstrate unity among the believers. When we share the bread and wine it is a powerful sign that God has accepted us and that we accept one another. It is a sign that we are part of one body, that we are a community.

A serving community

We all have specific gifts that God gives us to exercise in the community of the church, and in the wider community. Whatever our gifts, every one of us is called to serve in a practical way. Normally, we will serve in those areas in which we are gifted, but you do not have to have a special gift to serve – you just need to do it! Often, we actually discover what we are gifted at by offering to serve in a number of different areas. As we serve we discover what we enjoy and are good at, and others recognise those things that we do well in. The way that we serve in church life is vital because it is so tangible. This is one area which you can really measure. It is sometimes hard to discern whether we are really growing in worship or discipleship, but it is very easy to tell whether or not we are serving – if you are not sure, just check the rota!

Serving makes you happy!

Research has revealed that people who live in areas that record high levels of informal voluntary activity in their neighbourhood enjoy better health, students achieve higher exam grades and their communities suffer fewer burglaries. This should not surprise us. Jesus said, *it is more blessed to give than to receive* (Acts 20:35). God has created us to be happiest when we are our most generous. Churches should be happy places!

We were placed on the earth to serve God, and we do this very largely by serving others. The Bible word for this serving is 'ministry', and every believer is called to be a minister. Any time you use your talents, your abilities, your background, your experiences to help somebody else, you are ministering. All of us are called to serve in this way. *If you are called to salvation you are called to serve!*

Jesus is our model in serving. He once told his disciples, *The Son of Man did not come to be served, but to serve, and to give his life as a ransom for many* (Matthew 20:28). We are to follow his example. The call of Christ upon all his disciples is to be servants! Each of us is to model ourselves on Christ's own example of servanthood.

Because we place such high value on serving we ask every church member to serve in a practical way on one Sunday each month. We also encourage church members to serve in some way outside the church. For example, part of my wider community is *parkrun*, and on most Saturday mornings you will find me in Poole Park with around 500 others doing a 5k run. Just turning up and taking part is good, but I have much more fun by also being involved in some way, and enjoy volunteering in different roles that help the event. Serving makes you happy!

committed to the

CI

Commitment #11:
We are committed to the city

We exist for the good of the city

Technically, Poole, Bournemouth and Christchurch is not a city, but demographically a city is any 'large & permanent settlement', which it certainly is. 'City' is therefore a helpful shorthand term to use for the place we live. Also, theologically we can see that God has purposes for the city. The story of the Bible is in many ways a tale of two cities, represented by Jerusalem and Babylon. As well as being actual places, Jerusalem represents spiritually the city of God, while Babylon represents opposition to God. The conclusion to the story is that Jerusalem prevails and Babylon is defeated. In our city we want to see Jerusalem lifted up and Babylon thrown down, which means we are here for the good of the city.

Wherever you are, be all there

It is often easy to imagine that God could really use us if only we were somewhere else! We imagine that if God moved us to the other side of the world we would sudenly become much more effective for the gospel than we are now; but we wouldn't – we'd be just the same! The thing is God has a plan and purpose for us, right here, right now. This means that we are to live all here, right now! We are called to be a blessing to our city, and we do that by loving and serving our city.

Distinct and connected

Because we are citizens of Jerusalem rather than Babylon we need to be clear about who we represent and what we stand for. This means we think differently about some things from other people, and we act differently. At times this will bring us into conflict with our city, because we value different things, but even in such circumstances our motivation must be love for our city. In fact, we would fail our city if we were indistinguishable from it. In the church our city is meant to see the city of Jerusalem, and turn away from Babylon.

While we are called to be distinct from our city we are not hostile to it. We are people who eagerly await the resurrection. Anything that claims to be Christianity but is in reality only a life philosophy for the here and now is fairly useless; if that is all Christianity is we may as well choose to follow any other philosophy that suits us. As Paul writes in 1 Corinthains 15:14, *"If there is no resurrection…our faith is in vain!"* What we are awaiting is resurrection life which means eternal transformation and reward for the people of God. We believe what it says in Revelation 21:4, *"He will wipe away every tear from their eyes, and death shall be no more, neither shall there be mourning, nor crying, nor pain anymore, for the former things have passed away."* This vision of what to come must captivate us!

In Christ, we are promised a great destiny and a mighty inheritance. Christianity strains towards this future, because we know it will be so much better. On the day that we step into the fullness of our inheritance the whole of creation will be liberated: *The creation waits with eager longing for the revealing of the sons of God…the creation itself will be set free from its bondage to corruption and obtain the freedom of the glory of the children of God* (Rom 8:19-21)

This is what we believe and hope for. We are not looking for the world to be made, 'a little bit better' but for radical transformation! But it is this very hope that keeps us grounded and connected in the present world. You see, we are not wanting to escape the world, but to see the world transformed! Right here, right now the church is to demonstrate something of what the new world will look like. This means we are not hanging on for heaven but are focussed on being here for the city.

Our aim is not to struggle through life, die and then go and float on a cloud somewhere. Our hope is in resurrection life – resurrection life that will be as solid and real as the here and now is solid and real – only more so!

Praying for the city like Jesus

When the disciples asked Jesus to teach them to pray he gave them what we now call 'the Lord's prayer' (Matt 6:9-13). As well as being a great model for prayer generally, this prayer teaches us how to pray for our city.

Our Father in heaven, hallowed be your name
Christians have the remarkable privilege of being able to call God our Father. We are completely secure in his love, and we have all the rights that come from being his children. This means that we want to 'hallow' his name – we want to demonstrate our love and respect for the Father and cause others in our city to do the same. We want to help people see that there is a bigger story being told than just the story of what is happening in their own lives – a story of our heavenly Father.

Your kingdom come, your will be done, on earth as it is in heaven
The kingdom of heaven is not about people going to heaven but about the rule of heaven coming to earth. The God of heaven is establishing his rule not just in heaven, but on earth as well and the church is where this is meant to be seen! We are good news for the city because we demonstrate what heaven is like!

The Lord's prayer shows us something of how this looks…

Give us this day our daily bread
In the church we know the provision of God and he is able to supply us with all we need. Our faith is in *God* – not in the financial system, our own ability to make money, or the government to look after us. When the people of Israel were in the wilderness God provided bread for them each day. In the same way we provide for God to feed us with whatever it is we need, be that material, spiritual or emotional. This attitude of faith in God speaks to our city about a different value system and a different confidence. It also makes us a generous people, because we know that in God the pot will never run dry.

Forgive us our debts, as we also have forgiven our debtors
The church is a place of mercy because we have received mercy. We are to live with an awareness of what it is to be a forgiven sinner. We are to be grateful rather than grumbling and forgiving rather than grudge bearing. God has reconciled us to himself and this means we can be those who bring reconciliation to others. This is good news for our city!

And lead us not into temptation, but deliver us from evil
We do live differently to the city around us, and purity really does matter. Living as a pure people is an essential part of our corporate identity and witness which speaks to our city about the purity of God. In the purity of our lives and the good fruit this produces we are be witnesses to the desirability of Jersualem over Babylon.

Because we pray for our city like this we are good news for the city. We want to commend everything commendable that happens here, and get involved in being a blessing wherever we can. This means church members are involved in serving the the city in different ways, whether it be as a school governor or trustee of a rehab centre. It also means we want to equip and encourage every church member to be a blessing to the city in whatever it is we work at and play at.

Matthew 6:9-13

" *Pray then like this:*

"Our Father in heaven, hallowed be your name.
10 Your kingdom come, your will be done, on earth as it is in heaven.
11 Give us this day our daily bread,
12 and forgive us our debts, as we also have forgiven our debtors.
13 And lead us not into temptation, but deliver us from evil."

committed to

PREAC

HOLY BIBLE

CHING

Commitment #12:
We are committed to preaching

Our kind of preaching…

At Gateway we really value preaching and teaching. Teaching from the Bible forms a significant part of our Sunday meetings, and there are many other settings in which teaching takes place. Because teaching is so significant it is worth taking some time explaining what we believe about it, especially as what we believe about preaching is shaped by other important matters, such as what we believe about spiritual authority and the roles of men and women.

Who leads Gateway Church?[4]

Ultimately, God does. We read in Acts 20:28 that it is God's church which was bought by Jesus' blood and which is led by Holy-Spirit-appointed leaders. Whatever else we say about church government at Gateway, we must always remember that Jesus is the true head of the church (Ephesians 5:23) and the true Senior Pastor (1 Peter 5:4).

Having said that, we need to recognise that God sets out some clear guidelines in the New Testament for how he wants his church to be governed. We read in Acts 14:23 that the apostles appointed teams of elders to lead the local church, and in Titus 1:5 that this was their priority in every town. The New Testament uses three different words to describe these church leaders:

- *Episkopos* which means 'overseer'
- *Presbuteros* which means 'elder'
- *Poimen* which means 'shepherd' or 'pastor'

These three terms appear to be interchangeable and we refer to the leaders of Gateway as *elders*.

The model of church leadership we see in the New Testament is of apostles appointing elders in every church, under the guidance of the Holy Spirit. These elders are then responsible for guarding, guiding and governing in their church. Elders are always appointed in the plural – a team of elders, not a one-man-band-pastor, are meant to have oversight of the local church. Elders are appointed in response to the anointing of God rather than as an act of human promotion. They are to act as fathers within the church, ensuring that there is real spiritual life and vitality in the congregation. The elder team are meant to set the pace in keeping the local church adventurous, pure and compassionate. Being an elder is a high calling, and those called to it will have to give account to God, but it is also a wonderful privilege.

What does being an elder led church mean when it comes to teaching?

The father-like role of an elder can be summarized in three words:

- Guarding: *himself, the flock, and doctrine* (Acts 20:28; 1 Timothy 4:16)
- Guiding: *the church like a shepherd his sheep* (1 Peter 5:2)
- Governing: *as a faithful steward* (1 Peter 5:2)

---

4   Thanks to Phil Moore, from Everyday Church London, for help with this section

Let's think what this might mean in the context of teaching in the local church.

It seems to me that the **first question** to ask here is whether there are some kinds of teaching that functions to guard, guide and govern, and so ought to be the preserve of elders, and other teaching which does not have this function? That this is the case seems to be fairly clear. For example, compare Hebrews 5:12, "You ought all to be teachers" with James 3:1, "Not many of you should become teachers." I don't think these two verses contradict one another – I think they are telling us that there are different kinds of teaching!

It seems reasonable to assume there is 'big-t' teaching (James 3:1; Titus 2:1) which is restricted to some in the church (elders), and 'small-t' teaching (Colossians 3:16; Hebrews 5:12; Titus 2:3), which all believers should aspire to. This is made especially clear from the instructions concerning teaching and eldership found in 1 Timothy and Titus:

- There is a clear connection between Timothy staying in Ephesus, and Titus staying in Crete, to <u>teach</u> and appoint elders who can also <u>teach</u>.
- Timothy, Titus and the elders they appoint are to teach true doctrine because there are those in both communities who are teaching false doctrine.
- That this teaching is the preserve of elders is reinforced by the instruction that those elders "who labour in preaching and teaching" are worthy of double honour. (1 Timothy 5:17)

The picture painted for us would indicate that having a non-elder doing this kind of doctrinal teaching would be exceptional – unthinkable even. The whole point is that elders need to be properly appointed in order that teaching might be properly conducted. This is 'elder-teaching', the preserve of elders. Yet there is other teaching that it is very appropriate for others to do, E.g., the older women are to teach the younger (Titus 2:3) – which is 'gifted-to-teach-teaching'.

While the ability to teach is a key qualification for elders, this does not mean that the elders will always necessarily be the 'best' (as our itching ears might define the term) teachers in the church. Or, in other words, elders are not appointed simply because they are the most knowledgeable, engaging or compelling public speakers, but because of the overall quality of their character and gift and their ability to father the congregation.

Following on from this, the **second question** to ask is what contexts require elder-teaching (that is authoritative doctrinal teaching), the purpose of which is to guard, guide and govern the church? Specifically (and this is the question which I am most often asked), what should be our expectations of the teaching on Sundays? Should it be elder-teaching or anyone-gifted-to-teach-teaching?

Assuming that gathering the church together in one place at one time is a legitimate thing to do and that teaching should play a significant part in that, then it seems to make sense to me that we should be aiming for teaching that is authoritative. This teaching is authoritative not only because of the authority of the teaching, but because of the authority of the person delivering it. Throughout the story of God's people, when God's people gather, it is always the head of the household who is responsible for teaching. Put another way, such teaching is part of the way that we guard, guide and govern the church – so it should be elder-teaching. Which is why it is normally one of the elders who teaches on a Sunday at Gateway.

What are some of the implications of arguing that Sunday teaching should be elder-teaching?

If our teaching on a Sunday was only topical or thematic it would make sense that anyone best qualified to speak on a particular theme or topic should do so. But we do not want to settle for this kind of teaching! Our normal pattern is that when the church is gathered together the requirement is for preaching that opens up the Bible and helps guard, guide and govern the church. We want our teaching to be well informed and well communicated but the most important thing is that we submit ourselves to the authority of the word of God.

For most of the week we live in a hostile world in which Jesus is not worshipped and adored. Our culture has drifted a long way from its Christian origins. In such a world it seems crazy not to maximize the 35 minutes of teaching we have on a Sunday to dig into the word of God and bring something really authoritative rather than merely entertaining. We simply do not have the time to not have big-t type teaching on a Sunday!

This means that we would not normally have someone who is not an elder preaching on a Sunday. However, sometimes we make exceptions to this general principle, but such exceptions would generally be for those who have the potential to become an elders. As the Bible instructs us that one qualification for the appointment of elders is that they "must be able to teach", it seems reasonable to assume that men who are being trained for eldership are given teaching opportunities.

Although we do not know the exact patterns and context in which doctrine was taught in the early church it seems likely that our Sunday services are analogous settings. (After all, there is evidence that they gathered on the 'Lord's day' for worship and teaching: Acts 20:7; 1Co 16:2; Rev 1:10) This would imply that our Sunday teaching should be big-t and conducted by elders. We live in an age when there is just as much false teaching around as Timothy and Titus found in Ephesus and Crete and there is just as much need for elders who teach God's truth faithfully. The New Testament expectation of elders having a particular responsibility to guard, guide and govern the church through sound teaching still applies.

A legitimate concern that might be raised here is that such a strong emphasis upon Sunday teaching being the preserve of the elders might undermine the new covenant promise of Jeremiah 31 that all God's people will be teachers. However, one obvious response to this is the book of Hebrews, which quotes and expounds Jeremiah 31 at length, yet clearly offers authoritative teaching itself. While all believers are meant to be teachers there is still an appropriate place for authoritative teaching!

All the elders at Gateway are men — is this by accident or design?!

As well as understanding that the Bible teaches us that churches should be led by elders, we also believe that the role of elder is limited to men. We think the biblical evidence for this is plain:

In all the scriptures that describe elders it is implicit that they are men.

What is generally implicit is made explicit in the instructions about the appointment of elders found in 1 Timothy and Titus.

Further support for this is found in the close biblical parallel between human families and the church. While it is clear that there were female heads of households (E.g., Lydia, Acts 16:15) where a man was present he was assumed to be head of the household (E.g., Acts 16:33).

This assumption is reinforced by the expectation in 1 Timothy and Titus that elders have demonstrated the ability to lead their families well. Elders should be taken from amongst the very best household leaders within the church (1 Timothy 3:1-7, Titus 1:5-9). We can see this in the way that these lists of qualifications all assume that the elder will be a man — for example, faithful to his wife and managing his household well — and the way that they say a husband can be disqualified for eldership by his wife's character but not that she be qualified for eldership by her character. This also appears to be reflected in the fact that the words the New Testament uses for *elder, overseer* and *pastor* are all masculine nouns in Greek.

As well as holding to these things we believe the Bible says about elders, we also believe the Bible teaches us that men and women are equal in value but have distinctions in role.
Often the debate about male and female roles in the church and home never gets past this point. In our culture we are used to equal meaning equal! When we talk about equality we tend to mean the right to have or do the same things. However, all of us know that there can be genuine equality between people, but not necessarily the right or ability to have or do the same things. This is obvious in some of the distinctions between men and women. For example, Grace and I are both equally our kids parents, but our contribution to their coming into the world was rather different!

We want to take the Bible seriously, so we believe that the pattern and shape of male and female relationships described throughout the Bible serves as a model for us. Despite the sin and failings of many characters in the Bible (especially men!) there is an underlying pattern of equality with difference which we see all the way through the Bible story, from Genesis chapter 1 onwards. In some way, this pattern of equality and difference also reflects the way in which God has revealed himself to us: He is Trinity and there is complete equality between the Father, Son and Holy Spirit. Yet there is also distinction in role. For example, it was the Son who came to earth and died on the cross; it is the Holy Spirit who fills us with power and assurance; it is the Father who adopts us into his family. The apostle Paul makes the link between the Trinity and us explicit in 1 Corinthians 11:3, where he states, "the head of every man is Christ, the head of a wife is her husband, and the head of Christ is God."

We really do believe in the equality of men and women at Gateway and want to see every church member fulfilling their calling in Christ Jesus and using all the gifts he has given us. However, this does not mean that all of us get to do exactly the same things. We believe that the Bible teaches us that in marriage the husband has a particular responsibility to lead his wife, and that elders – who are men – fulfill a similar role in the church.

Let me illustrate this…

A domestic illustration

Many of the points I am making in this paper are helpfully clarified when the nature of relationships in the church are compared with how things should be in the family home. I think this is a good way to read the story, as the model given in the scriptures of the role of elders is that of heads of households – eldership is a fathering role.

For example, in my home there is a genuine conviction about our equality – that all six of us have equal standing and value before God. However, although we are equal in value, we are different! There are things I know and can do that my daughters don't and can't; but each of my daughters know and can do things that I don't, and in such instances can function as my teacher.

At the same time I have a God-ordained responsibility as head of the household and have primacy of responsibility for, and authority over, the household. This fact is not undermined by the fact that my daughters are cleverer than me, and know things I do not. Nor is their opportunity to further increase their learning undermined by my authority over them. There is also a sense in which leadership responsibility can shift between us – when I am away from home, the primary authority rests with Grace; when Grace is not present it rests with our oldest daughter; and so on.

When guests come to our house, the whole family is engaged in welcoming and entertaining those guests, but there is in some sense a particular responsibility upon me, as leader of the household, to set the tone for that welcome and entertainment, to guard the safety of the house, and to take the lead vocally in certain aspects of our hospitality. This doesn't undermine the other members of my family, or belittle their contribution, but helps us to run our home in a healthy way.

If this domestic pattern is a biblically faithful one (as I believe it to be!) then it does help illuminate the role of elders in the church.

If the teaching on Sundays is normally done by the elders, what about teaching in settings other than Sunday services?

In settings where teaching is thematic and topical rather than doctrinal there is a greater appropriateness for non-elders (both men and women) to be involved. An obvious example of this would be a series of special interest seminars being run at church. In such a case speakers would be chosen based on their expertise and experience in a particular area; and it would be clear that their teaching was not doctrinally determinative for the church.

Also, as already explained, we want to encourage *everyone* in the church to engage in gifted-to-teach teaching as appropriate.

Where does this leave us – and you?

If you are troubled by what we believe about teaching, we understand – let's talk! Our desire is to honour men and women equally and to encourage every disciple of Jesus to use their gifts appropriately. We do have clear, biblical, reasons for believing what we do about the role of elders though. This might at times mean we appear to be on the wrong side of what our culture expects, but we would rather be wrong on that, and faithful to what we believe God demands of us. We hope you will join with us in this.

We don't want to divide over these things, but we do want there to be clarity about our beliefs, why we believe them, and the practical out-workings of those beliefs. Our desire is to be as faithful to what the Bible teaches as we can be. We recognise that we will not always get this right, but this is an honest attempt to set out what we believe the Bible requires of us.

It is likely that your response to this will fall into one of three broad categories:

You just plain disagree with our position

If this is where you end up, please be really honest about why you disagree with us. Is it genuinely because you think we have misinterpreted the Bible, and have solid reasons for backing that up? Or is it more that you just don't like where we land because of what your culture and personal preference has taught you? That is an important distinction!

If this is a significant area of disagreement between us, it may be that you would be better off joining a different church. If this is the case, God bless you! However, it may be that while disagreeing with us you still want to be part of Gateway and are willing to submit to the leadership of the elders. In this case, great – you're more than welcome! All we would ask is that you do not vocalise your disagreement with us in a way that would cause division or confusion within the church.

You agree that we are probably on the right track biblically, but still don't much like our position

If this is where you end up, then please seek God's grace with real humility and a pure heart and ask him to help you submit your preferences to his perfect will. It is much better to submit than to kick against the goads! And please stick with us – it's great having you around!

You agree with our position

Great – we're so thrilled! Let's get busy together doing the work that Jesus has called us to!

Thinking About It

Below are a series of questions arising from everything we have looked at. This is not a test, but thinking about these questions will help clarify for you areas where you need to grow spiritually, and highlight things you might want to talk about with us. Take your time, and let the Spirit work in your heart as your think about these things.

Have you been baptised in water? When & how?

Have you been baptised in the Spirit? When & how?

List the areas in which you have experienced spiritual growth recently:

List the areas in which you need to see more evidence of spiritual growth:

In your experience, what are the best and worst things about being part of the church family?

Describe how your attitude to your money and possessions has changed since you became a Christian:

For each of the following pairs of statements, mark where you come on a scale of 1 to 10

I do not understand grace	1 2 3 4 5 6 7 8 9 10	Grace is my chief motivation in life
I often wrestle with feelings of guilt or inadequacy	1 2 3 4 5 6 7 8 9 10	I know that God's grace is sufficient for me in every circumstance
I have no confidence that my salvation is secure	1 2 3 4 5 6 7 8 9 10	I know I am a sinner saved by grace and nothing can remove me from God's love
I constantly struggle with sin issues in my life	1 2 3 4 5 6 7 8 9 10	By God's grace I am living a life that is increasingly sanctified
I find it difficult to praise and worship God	1 2 3 4 5 6 7 8 9 10	I am overwhelmed by God's grace to me and must express it!
I don't really think my sin can ever be dealt with	1 2 3 4 5 6 7 8 9 10	I know that Christ Jesus has born my sin on the cross
I have little sense of assurance that God is my Father	1 2 3 4 5 6 7 8 9 10	I know that God is, 'Abba, Father'
I have never truly repented of my sin	1 2 3 4 5 6 7 8 9 10	I have experienced the total forgiveness of God
I am very undisciplined about reading the bible	1 2 3 4 5 6 7 8 9 10	I am very disciplined about reading the bible
I rarely experience God speaking to me through his word	1 2 3 4 5 6 7 8 9 10	I often experience God speaking to me through his word
I find it very hard to participate in meetings	1 2 3 4 5 6 7 8 9 10	I love to participate in meetings
I find it very difficult to talk to others about my faith	1 2 3 4 5 6 7 8 9 10	I find it very easy to talk to others about my faith
I have little commitment to the church	1 2 3 4 5 6 7 8 9 10	I am fully committed to what the church is and does
I would rather no-one ever asked me any questions	1 2 3 4 5 6 7 8 9 10	I deliberately make myself accountable to other believers
I don't really feel attached to the church body	1 2 3 4 5 6 7 8 9 10	I feel fully connected to the church body
I don't really understand the vision of the church	1 2 3 4 5 6 7 8 9 10	I am passionate about the vision of the church
I don't really care about church planting	1 2 3 4 5 6 7 8 9 10	I am passionate to see the gospel advance

I hate it when a new person sits in my seat on a Sunday!	1 2 3 4 5 6 7 8 9 10	I have a great desire to see new people join us and for the church to grow
I am not at all sure Gateway is where I belong	1 2 3 4 5 6 7 8 9 10	I know that Gateway is definitely my spiritual home
I am not sure what 'the bride of Christ' means	1 2 3 4 5 6 7 8 9 10	I am passionate about the bride of Christ
I find it difficult to open up to other people	1 2 3 4 5 6 7 8 9 10	I always share my joys and sorrows with others
I never invite people to my home	1 2 3 4 5 6 7 8 9 10	I regularly practice hospitality
I do not want to be part of a small group	1 2 3 4 5 6 7 8 9 10	I am fully committed to fellowshipping with others in a small group
I don't feel I have any close friends at church	1 2 3 4 5 6 7 8 9 10	There are many people to whom I am close at church
I am easily distracted from going to church	1 2 3 4 5 6 7 8 9 10	Sunday mornings are a highlight of my week
I feel no differently about other Christians than I do about anyone else	1 2 3 4 5 6 7 8 9 10	I am intensely loyal to my church family
For me, the Lord's Supper is just a strange religious ritual	1 2 3 4 5 6 7 8 9 10	The Lord's Supper is a rich and meaningful experience for me
I don't have a clue what it means to be part of Newfrontiers/Commission	1 2 3 4 5 6 7 8 9 10	I am excited to be part of a dynamic church planting movement like Newfrontiers/Commission
So long as someone else gets stuff done around here I'm happy	1 2 3 4 5 6 7 8 9 10	I am deeply committed to serving and giving in this church family
I have no idea how much money I have in the bank	1 2 3 4 5 6 7 8 9 10	I keep a close track of my finances
I am burdened by debt	1 2 3 4 5 6 7 8 9 10	I am debt free
I do not yet practice tithing	1 2 3 4 5 6 7 8 9 10	I consistently give away in excess of the tithe
My finances are a constant source of anxiety to me	1 2 3 4 5 6 7 8 9 10	I am trusting God to supply all my needs
Whenever I get some extra money it simply disappears	1 2 3 4 5 6 7 8 9 10	Whenever I get some extra money I give it away or save it
I never think about the eternal significance of my money and possessions	1 2 3 4 5 6 7 8 9 10	I intentionally look to invest in heavens bank

Left statement	Scale	Right statement
I incline towards hoarding and miserliness	1 2 3 4 5 6 7 8 9 10	I love to be generous with the things God has given me
Special 'Faith Days' at church scare me	1 2 3 4 5 6 7 8 9 10	I love to push the limits of faith in my giving
I inevitably find there is too much month at the end of the money	1 2 3 4 5 6 7 8 9 10	I end every month still in the black
I never review my regular outgoings (mortgage/ rent, utility bills, etc.)	1 2 3 4 5 6 7 8 9 10	I regularly review my regular outgoings & seek out the best deals
I am trapped by the tyranny of things	1 2 3 4 5 6 7 8 9 10	I have deliberately chosen a simple lifestyle
My giving to the church is erratic	1 2 3 4 5 6 7 8 9 10	My giving is consistent and regular
I have no idea what my gifts are	1 2 3 4 5 6 7 8 9 10	I am very clear about my gifts
I rarely use my gifts to serve the church	1 2 3 4 5 6 7 8 9 10	My gifts are regularly used to serve the church
I do not have the gift of tongues	1 2 3 4 5 6 7 8 9 10	I speak in tongues every day
I have little expectation of God speaking directly to me	1 2 3 4 5 6 7 8 9 10	I expect God to speak to me, through various means
I come to church to be served by others	1 2 3 4 5 6 7 8 9 10	I come to church to minister to others
I am suspicious of leaders	1 2 3 4 5 6 7 8 9 10	I am committed to following the lead of the elders
I am too busy to serve others	1 2 3 4 5 6 7 8 9 10	I work hard at keeping myself available for others
When asked to serve I respond grudgingly	1 2 3 4 5 6 7 8 9 10	I love to serve because of my gratitude to God
When asked to do something I rarely see it through properly	1 2 3 4 5 6 7 8 9 10	When asked to do something I am faithful in doing it

Recommended Reading

If you would like to do some more study on the things discussed in this course we would recommend you read:

Surprised by the Power of the Spirit by Jack Deere
This book is an excellent, biblical, study of the reality of the work of the Holy Spirit. If you have questions about the place of spiritual gifts in today's church, this is a great place to start.

The Volunteer Revolution by Bill Hybels
Hybels sets out the vision for getting involved in serving in the church. If you can read this and not get excited about serving you might not have a pulse!

What's The Difference? By John Piper
One of the issues that most often troubles people is what we believe the Bible teaches about the differences between men and women. This little book helpfully sets out some of the issues.

God's Lavish Grace by Terry Virgo
With biblical and personal examples Terry explains what it means to enjoy the grace of God and to live a grace-filled life. This is a book to read with a smile!

Chosen By God by RC Sproul
The doctrines of election and predestination can seem confusing, but this is an excellent book that helps untangle some of the knots.

The Treasure Principle by Randy Alcorn
A very small book that packs a big punch! Alcorn challenges us to ensure our hearts are oriented in the right direction, so that the way we handle our money and possessions brings glory to God.

The Money Secret by Rob Parsons
Practical budgetting advice that anyone would benefit from following, told in the form of a parable.

The Gift of Giving by RT Kendall
In this book Kendall answers many of the questions people have about giving in general, and tithing in particular.

Why Church Matters by Joshua Harris
A short book, in the same series as The Treasure Principle which helps clarify the significance of the local church.

9 Marks of a Healthy Church by Mark Dever
A more indepth study of how the local church should function.

The Radical Reformission by Mark Driscoll
One pastors account of engaging with culture while building a church.

Desiring God by John Piper
A Christian classic, that teaches us to find our deepest joy in God.

Design and layout by

Made in the USA
Charleston, SC
16 April 2014